First World War
and Army of Occupation
War Diary
France, Belgium and Germany

61 DIVISION
Divisional Troops
308 Brigade Royal Field Artillery
1 January 1916 - 27 January 1916

WO95/3044/2

The Naval & Military Press Ltd
www.nmarchive.com
Published in association with The National Archives

Published by

The Naval & Military Press Ltd

Unit 10 Ridgewood Industrial Park,

Uckfield, East Sussex,

TN22 5QE England

Tel: +44 (0) 1825 749494

www.naval-military-press.com

www.nmarchive.com

This diary has been reprinted in facsimile from the original. Any imperfections are inevitably reproduced and the quality may fall short of modern type and cartographic standards.

© Crown Copyright
Images reproduced by permission of The National Archives, London, England, 2015.

Contents

Document type	Place/Title	Date From	Date To
Heading	WO95/3044/2		
Heading	308th Brigade R.F.A. 1915 Sep-1917 Jan Bde Broken Up		
Heading	War Diary 308th Bde R.F.A. Volume 3 (Vol 1& 2 enclosed May June) July 1st-July 31st 1916		
Miscellaneous	Messages And Signals		
Heading	War Diary Of The 2/4th South Mid. (How.) Bde. R.F.A. From January 1st,1916 To January 31st, 1916.		
War Diary	Writtie	01/01/1916	31/01/1916
Heading	War Diary Of 308th Bde RFA Late 2/4 S.M From 21st May 1916 To 31st May 1916 (Volume 1)		
War Diary		21/05/1916	31/05/1916
War Diary	B.E.F.	01/06/1916	13/06/1916
War Diary	In The Field	13/06/1916	29/06/1916
Miscellaneous	Appendix A Instructions for Enterprise Night of June 20/21 1916		
Miscellaneous	Appendix B O.C Lieut Group. R.f.a.		
War Diary	In The Field	01/07/1916	16/07/1916
War Diary	Laventie	16/07/1916	31/07/1916
Miscellaneous	Operations 4th/5th July		
Miscellaneous	Appendix A		
Diagram etc	Diagram		
Miscellaneous	Amendment 6 Time Table		
Miscellaneous	Programme For T. Ms		
Miscellaneous	Diary Of Operations	19/07/1916	19/07/1916
Miscellaneous	Appendix B Time Table		
Heading	War Diary 308 Art Bde Aug 1st-Aug 31st 1916 Volume 4		
Heading	War Diary Of 308th Bde R.F.A. From 1st Aug 1916 To 31st Aug 1916 (Volume IIII)		
War Diary	In The Field	01/08/1916	31/08/1916
Heading	War Diary 308th Art Bde Sept 1-30 1916 Vol V		
Heading	War Diary 308 Bde R.F.A. From 1st Sept 1916 To 30th Sept 1916 (Volume IV)		
War Diary	Laventie	01/09/1916	30/09/1916
Miscellaneous	Appendix A Instructions for Enterprise Night of 6/7th Inst. Sept 1916		
Miscellaneous	Operations-6/7th Sept.1916		
Miscellaneous	Appendix B. Nominal Roll of officers 61 Div. Art.		
Heading	War Diary 308 Art Bde Oct 1-31-1916 Vol 6		
Heading	War Diary Of 308 Bde R.F.A. From 1st Oct 1916 To 31st Oct 1916 (Volume VI)		
War Diary	Laventie	01/10/1916	01/10/1916
Miscellaneous	Instructions For Enterprise Night Of 1/2nd October 1916		
War Diary	Laventie	02/10/1916	07/10/1916
Miscellaneous	Messages And Signals		
Miscellaneous	Operation Order by Lieut Colonel F.H. Hilder for Night of 7th/8th Octr 16	07/10/1916	07/10/1916
War Diary	Laventie	06/10/1916	31/10/1916

Heading	War Diary 308th Bde 1-30 Nov 1916 Vol VII		
Heading	War Diary Of 308 Bde R.F.A. From 1st Nov 1916 To 30 Nov 1916 (Volume VI)		
War Diary	Laventie	01/11/1916	30/11/1916
Operation(al) Order(s)	61st Div Artillery Order No:21	17/11/1916	17/11/1916
Map	Map		
Miscellaneous	Table Of Reliefs To Be Carried Out On Night 18th /19th		
Operation(al) Order(s)	61 Div Art. Order No. 22	20/11/1916	20/11/1916
Operation(al) Order(s)	61 Div Art. Order No. 23	21/11/1916	21/11/1916
Operation(al) Order(s)	March Order No 5		
Operation(al) Order(s)	308th Brigade March Order No 3	22/11/1916	22/11/1916
Operation(al) Order(s)	308th Brigade March Order No 4	23/11/1916	23/11/1916
Heading	War Diary 308th Bde R.F.A. From 1st December 1916 To 31st December 1916 (Volume VIII)		
War Diary	In The Field	01/12/1916	31/12/1916
Miscellaneous	308 Brigade R.F.A.		
Heading	War Diary 308th Bde R.F.A. Mon Jan 1st-Jan 31st-1917. Vol IX		
War Diary	In The Field	11/01/1916	27/01/1916

WO 95/3044/2

61ST DIVISION

308TH BRIGADE R.F.A.

~~MAY 1916 - JAN 1917~~

1915 SEP — 1917. JAN

BDE BROKEN UP

Vol III
[1 and II]

CONFIDENTIAL   61 Div

WAR DIARY

308th Bde R.F.A.

VOLUME 3 (VOL 1 & 2 enclosed)
                    MAY   JUNE

July 1st — July 31st

1916

ALSO 2/4 Sth/Mid Bde 1/1/16 to 31/1/16

"A" Form. Army Form C. 2121.
MESSAGES AND SIGNALS.

TO D. By. 3th H.A.B.

Sender's Number: B/84
Day of Month: Seventeenth
AAA

In addition to the points given you to fire on the programme you are allotted 150 rounds Battery to fire in support line from N.14.a.8½.½ to N.14.c.½.5¾ during phases C E & 1 and K

From: Centre Group

"A" Form.
MESSAGES AND SIGNALS.

Army Form C. 2121.

Secret

TO D/306

Sender's Number: B 83
Day of Month: Seventeenth

AAA

In addition to previous 1 round every few minutes in replacement of the machine gun fire on the front line from N14a 6¾ . 1¾ to N14c 2⅔ 7 during phases C E G 1 K was allowance of ammunition 100 rounds per battery exclusive of fire on machine gun emplacements Z

Army Form C. 2118

WAR DIARY
or
INTELLIGENCE SUMMARY
(Erase heading not required.)

Instructions regarding War Diaries and Intelligence Summaries are contained in F. S. Regs., Part II. and the Staff Manual respectively. Title Pages will be prepared in manuscript.

Place	Date	Hour	Summary of Events and Information	Remarks and references to Appendices
			CONFIDENTIAL WAR DIARY OF THE 2/4th SOUTH MID. (HOW.) BDE. R.F.A. From JANUARY 1st, 1916 to JANUARY 31st, 1916. Writtle, 31.1.16.	

1875 Wt. W593/826 1,000,000 4/15 J.B.C. & A. A.D.S.S./Forms/C. 2118.

WAR DIARY
or
INTELLIGENCE SUMMARY

(Erase heading not required.)

Army Form C. 2118

Place	Date January 1916	Hour	Summary of Events and Information	Remarks and references to Appendices
WRITTLE			Reference 1" O.S.Map, Sheet No.30.	
	1st		Camp visited by MAJOR GENERAL R.BANNATINE ALLASON, C.B., G.O.C., 61st(S.M.) Division. aat	Battery Training includes Lectures
	2nd		Church Parade, Stables and Medical Inspection. MAJOR S.R.FIELD proceeded to LARKHILL for Course of Instruction on 4.5" Howitzer. MAJOR A.A.TORRENS assumes command of the Bde. aat	Gun Drill Miniature
	3rd		Battery Training. 2/Lt.L.G.LYSTER returned to duty. aat	Rifle Practice,
	4th		do. aat	Battery
	5th		do. aat	Manoeuvres,
	6th		Arrival of 24 recruits from the 3rd Line. WHITE CITY, BRISTOL. Battery Training.	Signalling,
	7th		do. 88 No.7 T.F.ARTILLERY TRAINING SCHOOL, WINCHESTER. Battery Trng.16	Physical
	8th		do. 9 Mark 10 G.S.Wagons 2/Lt.L.G.LYSTER proceeded to Larkhill. aat	Drill,
	9th		2/Lt.C.H.WILKINS and 2/Lt.E.MARTIN (late of B:E:F.) reported for duty. Battery Trng.	Battery Staff
			Church Parade, Stables, Medical Inspections. 2/Lts.N.C.BARNES, H.L.WILSON, J.G.KING,	Instruction,
			and C.S.GALLINGHAM, proceeded to LARKHILL for Course of Instruction on aat	Driving
			4.5" Howitzer.	
	10th		B.S.M. MACKEY M.J., No.18751, from 19th Reserve Battery, R.F.A. reported for duty as aat	Drill,
			Brigade Sergeant Major. Battery Training.	Equitation,
	11th		Battery Training. aat	Harness
	12th		do. aat	Cleaning,
	13th		2/5th BATTERY inspected by G.O.C.DIVISION. aat	Veterinary,
	14th		do. CAPTAIN G.L.PAIN proceeded overseas for Course of Instruction. aat	Stables &
	15th		do. 2/LT.G.CALM proceeds to ORDNANCE COLLEGE, WOOLWICH, on course of aat	Kit
			Instruction. LIEUT. M.W.HOLMES returns to duty from Sick Leave.	Inspections
	16th		Church Parade, Stables, and Medical Inspection. aat	&c.
	17th		Battery Training. aat	
	18th		do. aat	
	19th		do. aat	
	20th		do. Arrival of two 5" B.L.How.Wagons & Limbers. aat	
	21st		do. aat	
	22nd		do. aat	
	23rd		Church Parade, Stables, and Medical Inspection. aat	
	24th		Arrival of four 90 m/m Guns. Battery Training. Sergeant INSTRUCTORS No.51575, Sgt.HOWE, aat	
			and 23146, Sgt. HIGGINS, reported for duty from No.7 T.F.ARTILLERY TRAINING	
			SCHOOL, WINCHESTER. 2/Lt.R.A.RUSSELL, 9th R.WEST KENTS.REGT. reports for aat	
			duty as Brigade Signalling Officer.	

Army Form C. 2118

WAR DIARY
or
INTELLIGENCE SUMMARY
(Erase heading not required.)

Place	Date	Hour	Summary of Events and Information	Remarks and references to Appendices
WRITTLE	January /16.			
	25th		Battery Training.	acts
	26th		Arrival of 6 Ride Horses. Battery Training.	acts
	27th		Battery Training.	acts
	28th		do. Captain H.A.BOUGHTON-LEIGH proceeds overseas for Course of Instruction.	acts
	29th		do. 2/Lt. S.L.BIBBY proceeds to LARK HILL for Gunnery Course.	acts
			2/Lt. E.W.TUNBRIDGE do.	acts
	30th		Church Parade, Stables and Medical Inspection.	acts
			MAJOR S.R.FIELD returns to unit, and assumes command of the Brigade.	
	31st		Battery Training, 2Lt. G.GALE returns to duty.	

Arthur C Towne

Comdg. 2/4th S.M.(H) Bde, R.F.A.
Major,

Writtle,
31.1.16.

CONFIDENTIAL

War Diary
of
308TH BDE RFA Note 2/4 SM
From 21st MAY 1916 to 31st MAY 1916

(VOLUME 1)

(May '16 to Jan '17)

WAR DIARY
of
INTELLIGENCE SUMMARY.
(Erase heading not required.)

Army Form C. 2118.

3084. 13'Bde. R.F.A.

Place	Date	Hour	Summary of Events and Information	Remarks and references to Appendices
AMESBURY	21/5/16		The 13 Brigade entrained by detachments at ~~Amesbury~~ Matrons en route for ~~Southampton~~ Southampton. Embarkation proceeded well & the boat (S.S. S.M. Miller) left at 7pm.	
	22/5/16		LE HAVRE was reached at about 4:30a.m. but the disembarkation did not commence until 8:30 a.m. (English time 9:30 a.m.) when the M.L.O. arrived. Owing to the very limited space on the quay for horses & particularly for vehicles disembarkation took a considerable time but it was completed about 12 noon. A fatigue party of 1 Officer, 3 N.C.O, & 50 men was left to clean up the ship & one casualty occurred on the voyage. A horse broke its leg through getting it over one of the partitions & had to be shot. The horse was then dropped overboard. While this horse was being shot the men all about to their horses but this did not appear to have been necessary as the other horses seemed in no way alarmed. After disembarkation the 13 Brigade proceeded to the DOCKS REST CAMP (N°5) where the night was spent. Strength of the 13 Brigade on entrainment at AMESBURY:-	

P.T.O.

WAR DIARY or INTELLIGENCE SUMMARY

(Erase heading not required.)

Army Form C. 2118.

Summary of Events and Information

Personnel / Horses / Vehicles

Unit	Officers	NCOs	O. Ranks	R.	R.D.	H.D.	Guns, limbers	wagons, limbered wagons	G.S.	Motor Vehicles
A.13"by	5	1	135	42	83	4	4	8	2	2
B.13"by	5	1	135	30	95	4	4	8	2	2
C.13"by	5	1	135	42	83	4	4	8	2	2
D.13"by	5	1	137	43	84	4	4	8	2	2
H.qrs	5	1	48	30	7	8	–	Baggage 1 cart	4	2
Total	25	5	590	187	352	24	16	33	12	10

The above figures include all A.S.C., R.A.M.C. + A.V.C. attached. The Interpreter + his horse are not included as these joined the 13 Brigade after arrival in France.

The 13 Brigade entrained in detachments at the GARE-MARCHANDISE – destination unknown.

Date	
23/5/16	BERGUETTE was reached by the first detachment at 6.50 a.m. and by the last detachment about 4 p.m. Here the Brigade detrained. The first detachment arrived had previously detailed fatigue parties in accordance with the requirements laid down in "Notes on Embarkation, Detrainment &c &c." These parties were employed as required in the above but the detrainment took a very considerable time, whereas
27/5/16	

WAR DIARY
INTELLIGENCE SUMMARY
(Erase heading not required.)

Army Form C. 2118.

Instructions regarding War Diaries and Intelligence Summaries are contained in F.S. Regs., Part II. and the Staff Manual respectively. Title pages will be prepared in manuscript.

Place	Date	Hour	Summary of Events and Information	Remarks and references to Appendices
			the later detachments detailed fatigue parties as required by the R.T.O. at the Station and by this means were able to detrain in a very much shorter time. This owed point to the fact that it is not advisable to detail parties in advance as required in "Notes on Embarkation &c." and that the method of detrainment and number of fatigue parties required depends on the accommodation of the particular Station & arrangements should therefore be left to the R.T.O. at the detraining point. One casualty occurred during the journey from HAVRE. A horse became alarmed when passing through a tunnel and caused a stampede in the truck. The frightened animal broke its head collar & bent the chain fastening the door. It then fell out on to the line and was killed instantly. The train was stopped and a party went back in search of the horse which was found lying across the rails. A party of French railwaymen came up and removed the carcase. No blame could be attached to the picquets who sat all that was possible to calm the animal. One of the picquets was thrown out on to the footboard with the horse and was with difficulty saved from falling on to the line also. After detraining the Brigade proceeded to billets which were about 6 miles	

Army Form C. 2118.

WAR DIARY
or
INTELLIGENCE SUMMARY.
(Erase heading not required.)

Instructions regarding War Diaries and Intelligence Summaries are contained in F.S. Regs., Part II. and the Staff Manual respectively. Title pages will be prepared in manuscript.

Place	Date	Hour	Summary of Events and Information	Remarks and references to Appendices
	25/5/16		From the Station.	
	26/5/16		Parades under Battery arrangements for Gun Drill, improvement in Horse lines, telephone communication etc.	
	27/5/16			
ST. YENANT	28/5/16		Lecture to Officers of the Division by Lt. Gen. Sir R.C.B. Haking K.C.B. at Hôtel de Ville.	
	29/5/16		A party composed as under:- Major E.M. Faure, Capt. James, Capt. Caldicott, Capt. Smith, Capt. Moss, 4 telephonists from H.Q.S, 6 gunners & 6 telephonists per Battery proceeded to Annequin for attachment to 33rd Div. Art. for a course of Instruction	
	30 & 31 5/16		— NIL —	

[Stamp: COL. CMDG. 31 MAY 1916 308th BRIGADE R.F.A.]

305 Bde R.F.A. 61
June 1916.
Vol 2

WAR DIARY
INTELLIGENCE SUMMARY
(Erase heading not required.)

Army Form C. 2118.

Place	Date 1916	Hour	Summary of Events and Information	Remarks and references to Appendices
B.E.F.	June 1-3		Nil.	
	4		2/Lt. J.G. King & 6 men attached to T.M. School, St. Venant. Twenty one men attached to this Brigade for T.M.	
	5		One before & five bombardiers of the 305 Art. Bde attached to this Brigade to take temporary charge of the party of T.M. men. Captains James, Endicott, Smith & Moo of A.B.C&D/Batteries respectively and 52 men returned to their Units from attachment to the 33rd Division. Remainder of Officers with the exception of 2/Lieut. Mearns Barnes proceeded for attachment to the 33rd Division for course of instruction.	
	6-7		Nil	
	8		Major E.M. Luce returned to the Brigade from attachment to the 33rd Division.	
	9		2/Lt. Mearns Barnes attached to 33rd Division for instruction.	
	10		Nil.	
	11		Officers & men attached to the 33rd Division for instruction returned to their Units.	
	12-13		The Brigade proceeded by section to take over part of line occupied by the 38th Division. The 308th Brigade formed part of the left-Fauquemont Group.	

(2)

WAR DIARY
INTELLIGENCE SUMMARY.
(Erase heading not required.)

Army Form C. 2118.

June 1916

Place	Date 1916	Hour	Summary of Events and Information	Remarks and references to Appendices
In the field	13-15		The Fifth Bde. for the first part of the Fifth Group. This Group was composed of A,B,C & D Batteries, 367 Brigade, A,B,C,D/Battery, 308th. Bde., C,D Battery, 158 Bde., D/Battery 159H. Bde., +C. Battery, 174th Bde. Lt.-Col. Turner was in command of the left group. Ten Batteries of this group were in the line none (6/30p.Bde.) in rear. Considerable difficulty was experienced at first with the communication owing to the fact that no telephone exchanges are issued to Batteries under four-your line exchanges to Hqrs. The twelve-line exchange now authorized for Brigade Hqrs. is not yet available. Private exchanges had been made by each battery but these had been considerable attention. A sixteen-line were provided & therefore required considerable attention. Officers were compelled exchange were required at Group Hqrs. Under existing conditions the Government issue of telephones is quite inadequate. Officers were compelled to subscribe from their own personal funds to purchase additional instruments.	
	16		"C" Battery 158 Bde. + 1 section 174 left the front ordered to their own Division.	
	16-17		On the 16th. evening was received from Hqrs. of the possibility of the Gas attack north that night. All units were, at about midnight a violent armed	

T2134. Wt. W708—776. 500000. 4/15. Sir J. C. & S.

WAR DIARY (3) June 1916

Army Form C. 2118.

INTELLIGENCE SUMMARY

Place	Date	Hour	Summary of Events and Information	Remarks and references to Appendices
	16-17		At All[?]more an officer & 2/E Battalion were immediately warned to stand to. However in about half an hour the fire passed over and at one time was it sufficiently strong to warrant a relieve.	
	17-18		On the following night a "S.O.S. gas" alarm was received from the Right Bat[talion] at 1.0 am. The warning was immediately passed to all Batteries who at once opened fire in accordance with Standing Orders. At 1.30 am the Inf= B'de Hd[?] reported all clear & firing ceased. The signal alarm appear to have come through Inf= B'de Hd gts but at no time caused the presence of gas be detected.	
	-17		One section D/307 & one section B/174 & D/159 left the Group. C/307 from next	
	-18		left the Group & joined the Right Group. Composition of Group now:- A/3 cr D/308 & A/3 & D/307.	
	19		Capt. McIvish C/300 attached to the Right Group from the 19th inst.	
	20-21		A copy of the orders for the enterprise of the night of the 20th & 21st inst is attached. Appendix "A". At about 10.15 pm the Germans opened heavy rifle fire & this died away at about 10.30 pm. Just before 10.30 pm a message was sent through from the 5th GLOUCESTERS that the Germans were	

WAR DIARY
or
INTELLIGENCE SUMMARY.

Army Form C. 2118.

June 1916

Place	Date	Hour	Summary of Events and Information	Remarks and references to Appendices
			attacking at "Jam Jar" & the Group Commander then ordered "Barrage Slaughterat". This was passed on to the Right Group & the Group AUSTRALIANS (on our left). Gave fire was received from the front line at 11pm. The Germans retained on our communication & support trenches with H.7 (Heut). As a rover of the forgoing the raid did not take place. It is rumoured that the report that the Germans were attacking arose from the fact that there was probably a round wire cutting party out. Undoubtedly there was no German attack. As there was no shelling or rifle firing at the time of the alarm the Group Commander asked for confirmation. This Forward Control Officer reported that the Germans were attacking and fire was then opened. Our firing appeared to be very effective. The Enemy was great deal of damage was done to hand been done to the German parapet. A copy of the Group Commander's Forward Control Officer's attached. Appendix B.	Appendix (?)
	23rd.		2/Lt. ff. King posted to Medium T.M. Bty with effect from 11th inst.	130.
	24th		From the 12th - 24th. this front was a quiet one, with very little firing. On the 24th. our artillery commenced a period of increased activity

WAR DIARY
INTELLIGENCE SUMMARY.

Army Form C. 2118.

June 1916.

Place	Date	Hour	Summary of Events and Information	Remarks and references to Appendices
	28th		Systematic day & night harassing fire & shelling of the Germans was carried out during A 12th Hour. Cooperated in this bombardment firing from Laventie on the 27th inst. A/308 did some registration work with aeroplane during the morning. Owing to a misunderstanding with reference to targets to be engaged the results were not very good. On the following day however excellent shooting was done. The enemy artillery shelled LAVENTIE during the day & we obtained buffering on AUBERS. The enemy Artillery were apparently searching for the 12" How. It would appear that the enemy had obtained very definite information as to the exact position of this How. as many shells fell within 100 yards of it. Some (a 5.9 which fortunately did not explode) within 3 feet. A message was received from an aeroplane which had located the flashes of the Noble Battery - and same concentrated on this front & the hostile shelling ceased. Copies of instructions for the enterprise night 28/29th are attached	Appendice A
	28/29			

WAR DIARY

INTELLIGENCE SUMMARY

June 1916.

Army Form C. 2118.

Place	Date	Hour	Summary of Events and Information	Remarks and references to Appendices
			During the three preceding days wire had been cut except open at one different points in the enemy's line. Infantry patrols reported that the wire had at some points in artillery fire cut off of the first 17 ft of it been properly cut. The raid was timed to start at 12 midnight. Previous to the Artillery bombardment the Infantry had left our trenches & gone over the parapet. The raiding party which consisted of one Company of the 4th Bn. Before reached the enemy's wire without mishap. Gaps in the wire had been practically unmoved by enemy during our move into position & this occasioned slight check. A fierce struggle ensued on enemy's parapet in which the enemy suffered heavily. The fight with bombs continued on enemy's front line until 1 A.M. when the signal was given to withdraw. Most of our casualties occurred during the return journey as the Germans established a very heavy barrage in No Man's Land, though this the raiding party had to pass. Our total casualties were 8 killed and about 37 wounded.	Appendix A
	29.		Just before midnight the enemy again started shelling LAVENTIE. One shell struck Group Headquarters and came through the roof not more than 6 feet above the place where 2 men were sleeping. These men were unhurt.	

Army Form C. 2118.

WAR DIARY
or
INTELLIGENCE SUMMARY.

June 1916.

(Erase heading not required.)

Instructions regarding War Diaries and Intelligence Summaries are contained in F. S. Regs., Part II. and the Staff Manual respectively. Title pages will be prepared in manuscript.

Place	Date	Hour	Summary of Events and Information	Remarks and references to Appendices
			In retaliation we shelled Aubers and the hostile fire ceased immediately. 2/Lt. G.H. Smith was observing in the front trenches when he was hit by a piece of our own shrapnel. Several complaints have been made as to the condition of the ammunition taken over from the outgoing Division. The fuzes are most irregular.	80.

W. Price

Col. Cmdg.
308th Brigade, R.F.A.

Very SECRET

Appendix A

INSTRUCTIONS FOR ENTERPRISE NIGHT OF JUNE ~~19/20~~ 20/21 1916

Ref. Brigade Trench
Map, Area K.

1. A Small raiding party from the Gloucesters will carry out a raid on enemy's trenches at ~~N. 19. a 6½. 9½.~~ N 13 c 7.0 on the night of the ~~19/20~~ 20/21 June.

2. Artillery and Trench Mortar (Medium) support will be carried out as per annexed programme.

3. Zero time 10-30 p.m.

4. Watches will be synchronised at 4 p.m., 6 p.m., 7 p.m., on the 19th inst by Telephone.

5. Capt Moss will act as forward control Officer in Communication with the Left Group Commander.

6. Constant reports as to the situation will be sent in by all Officers to the Left Group Commander.

7. ACKNOWLEDGE.

18/6/16

Sent out by Orderly at

	Copy No.1.	R.A. 61st Division.
"	No.2.	184th Inf. Bde.
"	No.3.	A/308.
"	No.4.	B/308.
"	No.5.	C/308.
"	No.6.	D/308.
"	No.7.	A/307.
"	No.8.	B/307.
"	No.9.	D/307.
"	No.10.	D.T.M.O.
"	No.11.	File.
"	No.12.	War Diary.

[signatures] Left Group

Section Fire 30" after 10.55

1ST STAGE ZERO - 1 MIN.

Bty.		Target.	Rate of fire	Ammn.	Total for Gun Sec.
A/307.		N.14a.7.2. to N.14 c. 9.9.	3 rounds gun fire	S.	12.
B/307.	(1Sec)	N.14.c.o.8.- N. 13 d.9.6½.	"	S.	6.
Do.	(1Sec)	N.19a.6½.8- N. 19 a.8½.9½	"	S.	6.
D/307	(1Sec)	N.19a.9.5 - N. 19 a.9½.6½.	10 secs.	H.E.	6.
B/308	(1Sec)	N.13 c.7½.1.- N. 19 a.8½.9½	5 secs	S.	12.
"	(1Sec)	N.19a. 6.9. - N. 19 a.7.8.	"	S.	12.
C/308	(1Sec)	N.14a. 8.4. - E. 14a. 5½.⅓.	3 rounds gun fire	½ H.E. ½ S.	6.
D/308.	(1Sec)	N.13.c.7½.1.- N. 19 a. 6.9.	10 Secs.	H.E.	6.
D/308.	(1Gun)	N.19 a. 3.2.	"	H.E.	6.
D/308.	(1Gun)	N.19 a. 4.5.	"	H.E.	6.
		2ND STAGE. 1 min - 10 mins.	sec.fire	½ H.E. ½ S.	54.
A/308.		N.19 a. 6.9. to N.19a.3½.6.	~~30~~ secs		
C/308.	(1 Sec)	N.13 c.8.1. to N.13 d.o.3½.	Sec.fire 10 secs.	"	54.
"	"	N.13 d.2.5. to N. 13 d.3½.4.	"	S.	54.
D 308.	"	as in 1st stage	Sec.fire. 30 secs.	H.E.	18.
~~D~~					
D.308	(1 Gun)	as in 1st stage	30 secs.	"	18.
~~B. 308~~	(1 Gun)	as in 1st Stage	"	S.	18.
B.307.		Do.	Bty fire 10 secs.	S.	54.
			"		
B.308.		Do.		S.	54.
D.307.		Do.	Bty fire 30 secs.	H.E.	18.
A.307.		Do.	Bty fire 10 secs	S.	54.
		3RD STAGE 11 mins - 15 mins.	Sec fire	½ H.E. ½ S.	10.
A. 308	(1 Sec)	N.19a.3.5. to N.19 a.4.7.	30 Secs.		
"	"	N.19.a.3⅓.1½. to N.19a.5½.7.	" "	" "	10.
C. 308.	"	N.13 d. ½.1½. to N.13 d.3½.4.	" "		10.
C.308.	"	N.13 d. 2.5. to N.13.d.3½.4.	" "	S.	10.
B.307.	"	N.14 a. 9.4.to N.14 a.6.1½.	" "	S.	20.
B.303.	"	N.13. c 9½.2½. to N. 13 d. ½.1¼.	" "	S.	18.
"	"	N.13c. 9½.2½. to N. 13 d. 2.1½.	" "	½ H.E. ½ S.	10.
D. 308.	"	N.19a. 9.5. to N.19 a.9½.6½.	Sec.fire.	H.E.	5.
" "	(1 Gun)	N.19 a. 3.2.	1 min.		
" "			1 min.	"	5.
" "	"	N.19 a. 4.5.	"	"	5.

Bty.	Target.	Rate of fire	Amm.	Total for Gun Sec.
D. 397. (1 Section)	N. 15 d. N. 1½.	Sec fire per 1 min.	H.E.	5

4TH STAGE   16 mins- 25 mins.

Targets as in 3rd Stage.

18 pr Guns.	Battery fire 5 secs. Section fire 10 " Gun fire 20 "
4.5" How.	Section fire 1½ mins. Gun fire

SECRET.

TRENCH MORTAR BATTERIES Y/35 and Y/61.

1. 1 Gun will fire on Point N. 13.d.8½-9.) These guns will
   1 "   "   "   "   N. 13.d. 2.7.   ) bombard the
   1 "   "   "   "   N. 14 a. 7½.3.   ) enemy's wire
) from zero to 10
) minutes.

2. 5 Guns will fire on the point of entry at N. 13.c.7.0.

   (a) From Zero to 7 Fire on enemy's wire. This is reported
       to extend from 60^X to 20^X in front of the parapet.

   (b) From 8 to 10 Fire on enemy's parapet. Range to be
       liberally estimated.

   (c) From 11 to 25. Fire on the work running from N.19a.9.5.
       to N. 19 a.9½. 6½.

3. Rates of fire As quickly as possible.

4. Lieut   Edell, R.F.A. and four Orderlies will report
   to the O.C. Gloucesters before zero time.

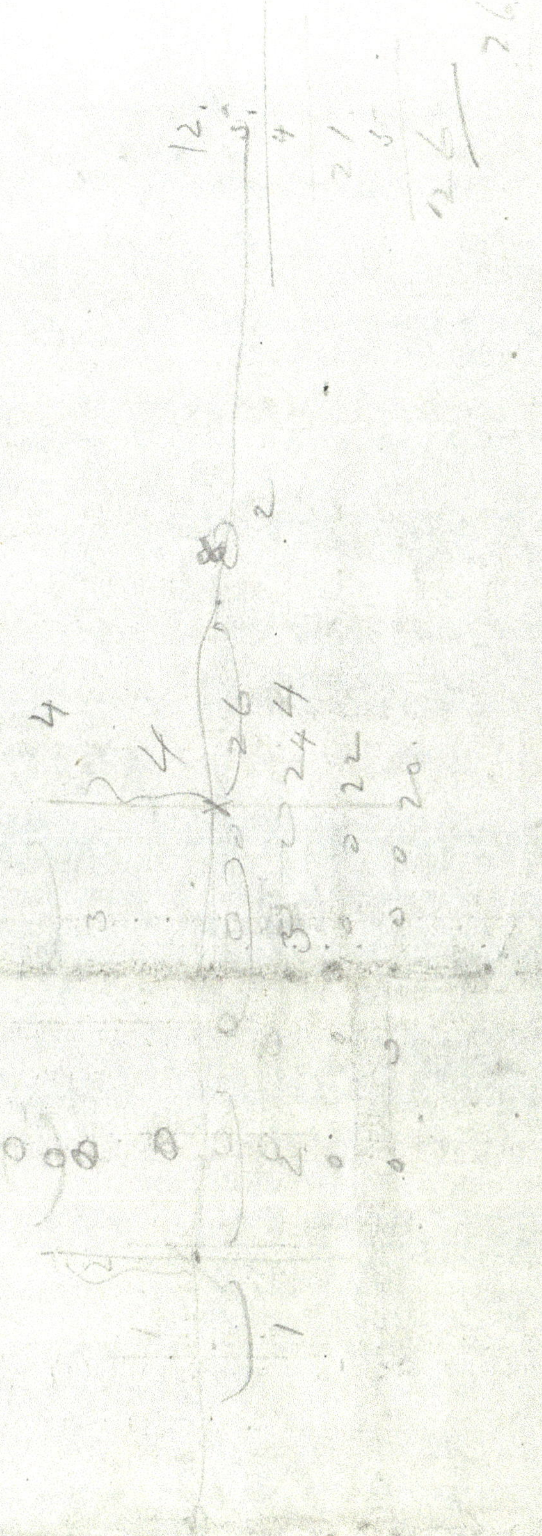

VERY SECRET

Ref. Brigade Trench Map
Area K.

Appendix A
Copy No. 13
28/6/16

INSTRUCTIONS FOR ENTERPRISE NIGHT OF 28/29TH INST.

1. A Company in the 184th Infantry Brigade will make an attack on P.2

2. The attack will commence at 12/15 am on the 29th inst.

3. Our Infantry will occupy the trenches for 40 minutes and will then return to their own trenches.

4. The bombardment will commence at midnight 28/29th inst and will be carried out in accordance with Table A and sketches A.B.C & D.

5. At 12/15 a.m. on the 29th inst a barrage of Fire will be directed against the line N.14.c.2.8½ to N.14.c.6½.3 to N.14.d.4.8 to N.14.a.9.5

6. Rates of Fire   –   0 to 0.20   Section fire 15 seconds (18 prs
                                                                                               (Hows
                           0.20 to 0.70   do   15 seconds (18 prs
                                                                                            1 minute (Hows
                           0.70 onwards   do   1 minute   18 prs
                                                                                                 1 minute . Hows

7. The fire of all Batteries will be continued until the order to stop firing is received from Group Headquarters. Reports from F.O.O's when they see red rockets being fired must be forwarded to Group Headquarters without delay.
   If reported before 12/15 am red rockets mean "Operations cancelled". If after 12/15 am it means Infantry are withdrawing and require support.
   If communication breaks down Batteries will decrease the rate of fire to section fire 1 minute, at 1/10 a.m., by which time it is expected our Infantry will have returned.

8. After "stop firing" all Batteries will stand by in case of counter-attack.

9. M.T.M. will co-operate as shown in Tables A.

10. Reports during the operations and immediately afterwards will be sent to Divisional Headquarters.

11. Watches will be synchronised at 7 p.m. 9/30 p.m. & 11 p.m. on the 28th inst.

12. Lieut.Dickinson will perform the duties of Forward Control Officer and will report to Col. Ames at 11/30 p.m. 28th inst.

13. ACKNOWLEDGE

Issued at

      Copy No. 1.61st Div. Art   Copy No. 8   B/307
         "   "   2.184 Inf. Bde   "   "   9   D/307
         "   "   3.A/308.   "   "   10   D.T.M.O.
         "   "   4.B/308   "   "   11   File
         "   "   5.C/308   "   "   12   War Diary
         "   "   6 D/308
         "   "   7 A/307

0.6 0.10 A 308 (4 guns)   F1 ½S ½HE   On front &
          C 308 (3 guns)   F4   "   support lines
          B 308 (4 guns)   F6   "   as at cT's
          D 308 (1 gun)   N13d 2.2 7½   "
          D 308 (1 gun)   N8d 4.1½   "

0.10 to 0.15 as above in addition except B/308
          B 308 (4 guns) N13d 5 7½ to N14c 1½ 8½
          A 307 (")   N14c 2/8½ to N14a 9.5
          B 307 (")   N14a 9.5 to N8d 4.1
          D 308 (1 gun) N14c ¾ 8½
          D 308 (1 gun) N14d 2.3 ½
          D 307 (")   N14a 9 4½
          D 307 (")   N14 b 2.8

0.15 - 0.20 Howitzers as above
          B 308 2 guns   F4
          B 308 (1 gun) N13d 5 7½ to
                         N13d 7½ 7½
          C 308 (3 guns) N14c 2 8 2
                         N14c 6½ 3
          A 307 (3 guns) N14a 9.5
                         to
          B 307 (4 guns) N14a 4.8
                         N14c 6 2 3
                         to
          A 308 (3 guns) N14d 4.8
                         F1
          A 308 (1 gun) N14a 9.5
                         N8d 4.1

0.20 - 0.70. as above except Howitzers
          D 307 (1 gun) N14c 1¼ 7¼
          D 307 (") N14c 2½ 5.4
          D 308 (") N14b 3.2 to N14b 4.3
          D 308 (") N14d 2½ 2
          D 308 (") N14b 3.0 to N14b 4 1¼

0.70 - onwards "Close Barrage"
          B 307 4 guns N14c 5½ 8.4 to N14a 9½ 2¼
          C 308 3 "   N14a 3.4.0 to N14c 4½ 7½
          A 307 3 "   N14a 8 3½ to N14a 9 1½
                Howitzer as from 0 to 0.20

O.C. Left Group. R.F.A.   Copy   Appendix B

I was detailed by O.C Left Group as forward Control Officer for the R.F.A. taking part in operation for the night of 20/21st June 1916. At 10.15pm the enemy opened very Heavy rifle & machine gun fire, assisted by light trench mortars. I was at this time with the Colonel Commanding the Right Battallion in Bay 48, and at 10-20pm an officer in shirt sleeves & a revolver in hand, rushed along the trenches shouting out "The enemy are attacking", and at the same time forcing men up to the fire step. The Colonel rushed out to see where the order had come from and who gave it, but there were so many men in the way that I feel certain he did not get hold of the officer who said, the Germans were attacking. I rushed out after the Colonel to try and gain some sort of information, but failed to trace where he had gone. I then rung up Battallion HQ and asked for Artillery to open fire as it was reported the enemy were attacking. I then got up on a fire step, & could not see any signs of the enemy, so tried to find the C.O to get information regarding the situation, but could not find him for some time, and as soon as I did, I phoned through for the Artillery to "Stop Firing", and after a lot of trouble due to cut wires, got my message through & the fire ceased. I could clearly see when looking over the parapet, figures moving towards our trenches. I heard "rumours" when leaving the trenches "That it was our own PATROL returning", but it may quite easily have been a small party of Germans, out cutting wire, in front of our trenches and the officer may have been quite right in the order he gave about the "Enemy attacking". Retaliation by the enemy was mostly with light guns and howitzers and Light trench mortars.

(sgd) J. W. Joss
Capt.
Forward Control Officer

Copy

Comdg Left Group 61st Div
Artillery.

To Brigadier General R.C. Coates D.S.O.
Comdg Div Artillery 61st Division.

I beg to forward report of the operations that took place on the night of the 20/21 June 1916. Capt. L.J. Moss. R.F.A's report is attached.

At about 10.15pm the Germans opened somewhat heavy rifle fire which died away about 10.20pm. Just before 10.30pm a report was received from Capt Moss that the Germans were attacking. As there was no rifle or gun fire at the time, I asked for the message to be repeated. On receipt of the message again I ordered "Fire on night lines" and fire was opened within a minute. Capt Moss then stated that the Germans were attacking at Drury Lane & I ordered "Barrage FAUQUINART." Communication with the front line then was broken. After repeated attempts to get through on two separate lines I sent Lt Macnamara to the Farm O.P. to try & get into communication with the front line by visual or telephone. He was unable to do so owing to the Germans having barraged the intervening ground between Capt Moss & the visual receiving station. Lieut W.Ealing earthed one end of the line and Capt Moss did the same at his end, and eventually the message got through to stop fire about the same time as the Infantry got the same message through. The officer who led the raid reported to me, that the wire had been cut & that the Germans parapet had been badly knocked about. This officer had apparently moved out from our line directly the guns opened fire. Capt Moss reports that our fire appeared very effective the shells fell at the correct range & burst at the right height.

21/6/16.

(Sgd) W.Furse Lt Col
Comdg Left Group

WAR DIARY
INTELLIGENCE SUMMARY.
(Erase heading not required)

Army Form C. 2118.

July 1916.

Place	Date	Hour	Summary of Events and Information	Remarks and references to Appendices
In the Lines	July 1916 1-4		Systematic shelling & day night back firing was continued. A copy of the orders for two enterprises in the night of the 4th/5th are attached. The house nightly rifle fire pl ace as usual from 10:0 – 10:30 The first raid was undertaken by "W" Company of the 7th Worcesters. A portion of this party succeeded in entering the German trenches and bombed several dugouts for a distance of from 30 – 40 yds. The main party however were held up in a wiring ditch just in one side of the enemy's parapet & there did not succeed in entering the trench. The enemy were apparently expecting an attack & had prepared bombing posts on each side and in rear of the Gap. Artillery fire as intended, their retaliation on wiring spot and fire was directed on wiring party. Casualties, 4 officers wounded, N.T. 2 killed & 25 wounded. The second raid was undertaken by 4th Gloster. There also crossed without being fired on. The scouts were practically the same as in the first raid. A small number entered the German trenches but the remainder were reported to have been held up by the narrowness of the Gap in wire. Casualties: officers 1 killed, 1 wounded, N.T. 12 killed & 40 wounded.	See Appendix "A" "A"

(2)

WAR DIARY

INTELLIGENCE SUMMARY

July 1916.

Army Form C. 2118.

Place	Date	Hour	Summary of Events and Information	Remarks and references to Appendices
		6.M.	Instructions were received that the batteries of the 307 Brigade, forming part of Left Group were to pull out during the night of 6/7th & 7/8th. Its position further south before they would form part of the new Right Group. The Division is now composed of the Right, Centre & Left Groups. The Left Group comprises the 308 Art B'gade complete.	
		9.10	On the night of the 9th & 10th. the enemy heavy shelled the emplacement of B/308 with 4.2". A direct hit at the gun pit caused damage to the slide, the spring buffer casing & the thread on elevating gear of range drum. As a result the gun was out of action. There were two other direct hits, one on a gun pit and one on a dugout, but these had both been vacated by the B/307 two days previously.	
		10	At about 6.30 am the enemy started heavy shelling of C/308 position. At first section salvos at one minute intervals were put out but as soon as the correct range was attained it apparently changed to Gun fire. The shelling lasted until about 8.30 am; approximately 150 S.g'shells were sent over. The firing was directed by a Boche plane and the wireless station	

(3)

WAR DIARY
INTELLIGENCE SUMMARY
(Erase heading not required.)

Army Form C. 2118.

July 1916

Place	Date	Hour	Summary of Events and Information	Remarks and references to Appendices
		10th	at Group Hd/rs picked up a front "Z. Bravo" immediately after the first direct hit. As a result of the shelling one gun only was damaged and that only slightly. One empty gun pit was badly smashed in. It is rather a curious fact that the two farmhouse occupied by 'C' Battery were absolutely blown to pieces. stones & other houses within 300 or 500 yards were untouched. All fifteen pits were lost. The flash of the hostile battery were located & reported to the flanks.	
	11th		Hostile Artillery were again active about 7 pm but did not shell this group. 1 narrows in Shanghi. 2 other ranks posted to A 308 and 2 O.R. to B 308	
	12th		3 O.R. posted to C 308. 3 O.R. to B 308.	
	13th		Hostile activity NIL. Wire previously cut not repaired.	
	14th		Wire cutting continued	
	15th		Wire cutting and drills continued. Very slight hostile activity.	
	16th		Lt. Col. HILL takes over command of "A" LEFT GROUP, composed of NEW 307 ART BDE. = C/308 – and 1st 3rd 5th & 7th Batteries R.F.A. and B/307 is the enfilade Battery affiliated to 183 Infantry Bde.	

WAR DIARY
or
INTELLIGENCE SUMMARY.
(Erase heading not required.)

Army Form C. 2118.

Place	Date	Hour	Summary of Events and Information	Remarks and references to Appendices
Laventie	16th		This Group H.Q. (the old LEFT GROUP) now became CENTRE GROUP, commanded by Lt Col Furse, and comprised A306 B305 C305 C306 D306 "O" "Z" D"RHA Group H.Q. remained in LAVENTIE. The "O" and "Z" RHA batteries went into wire-cutting positions as also were B/305 and C/305.	
	17		Situation quiet. Batteries registered their new zones and some wire-cutting was done. By this time the enemies wire is in a very bad condition having been cut through all along the line by our fire	
	18		Enemy bombards RUE TILLELOY on which road our O.Ps are situated. A direct hit on the dugout at BERKELEY O.P. caused the following casualties:- 2 Officers and 3 O.R. Killed further casualties were caused by the officers in the O.Ps on either side coming to render assistance, in H.E. 4.2 burst in the working party causing the following casualties:- 1 Officer killed 2 wounded None of these casualties belonged to this Brigade.	

WAR DIARY
or
INTELLIGENCE SUMMARY.
(Erase heading not required.)

Army Form C. 2118.

July 1916

Place	Date	Hour	Summary of Events and Information	Remarks and references to Appendices
LAVENTIE	19		Heavy artillery bombardment commencing at 11am including with Infantry attacks from 6pm onwards. German front line entered at several places. Casualties heavy, caused by MACHINE GUN fire. Enemy retaliation principally on communication trenches and on B/308, 32 B/y and 36 B/y both the latter of the 8th Division. These batteries continued in action. Artillery communication very good.	See Appendix "B"
	20		1st E.S. OSTLER transferred from H.Q. Staff to C/308 B/y with effect from 13th inst. 1st S.F. EMPSON posted from C/308 to H.Q. Staff as ADJUTANT with effect from 13th inst. 2nd N.C. BARNES transferred from H.Q. Staff to D/308 B/y with effect from 13th inst. 2nd K.W. MEALING posted (from attached) to H.Q. Staff as ORDERLY OFFICER. Grants programme to keep enemy wire open and prevent trenches in parapet from being repaired.	

WAR DIARY or INTELLIGENCE SUMMARY.

Army Form C. 2118.

July 1916

Place	Date	Hour	Summary of Events and Information	Remarks and references to Appendices
LAVANTIE	21		Very little aerial activity. Firing carried out to keep open wire gaps. Retaliation very feeble.	
	22		The enemy has made some attempt to repair his parapet and wire. Sandbag ladders formed not, and wire in coils being noticed as new. Some activity by hostile artillery was soon silenced by our guns.	
	23		Situation quiet. Day and night firing carried out at varying intervals.	
	24th		Lt Col HILDER took command of CENTRE GROUP vice Lt Col FURZE. Groups were rearranged into RIGHT & LEFT GROUPS. Lt Col HILDER being in command of the LEFT GROUP.	
	25th		No aeroplane activity. The enemy made attempts to repair wire but all points were fired on and wire again destroyed.	
	26th		A little aerial activity but no heavy shelling.	
	27th		A repealing round for 2 mm per battery commenced at Bde H.Q.	
	28th		C/308 again shelled out of their position casualties: 2 Bdrs & 2 gunners wounded.	

Army Form C. 2118.

WAR DIARY
or
INTELLIGENCE SUMMARY.
(Erase heading not required.)

Instructions regarding War Diaries and Intelligence Summaries are contained in F. S. Regs., Part II. and the Staff Manual respectively. Title pages will be prepared in manuscript.

Place	Date	Hour	Summary of Events and Information	Remarks and references to Appendices
LAVENTIE	29 30 31		Situation very quiet. Work on O.Ps progressing and visual signalling organisation being improved. Inspection of wagon lines by G.O.C. R.A. very satisfactory.	

W. Peace Lt Col
R.A. 13th Divn
Comdg 303

OPERATIONS 4th/5th JULY.

Apendix 'A'

1. 12 m.n.   The drill commenced to time.
2. 12.3 a.m. (2Lt.
              (Mealing telephoned from Adance Centre our Infantry over trenches.
3. 12.4 "   Informed Bde. Major (2).
4. 12.14"   Bristol O.P. (A/307) reports enemy slightly shelling our trenches.
5. 12.15 "   Informed Bde. Major (4)
6. 12.25 "   Bristol O.P. (A/307) reports heavy shelling of our front trenches.
7. 12.26 "   Informed Bde. Major (6).
8. 12.27 "   Australians rang up offering assistance. Thanked them but said "not yet".
9. 12.32 "   Two red rockets reported from N 8. 1. (Bristol O.P. report).
10. 12.33 "   Bde. Major informed (9).
11. 12.32 "   Bde. Major instructed us to get on to Snowdon to find out which portion of our trenches was being shelled.
12. 12.38 "   2Lieut. Mealing reports that shelling of our trenches was at N 8 c 9.7 and that 5.9's (apparently from AUBERS) were falling on RUE TILLELOY.
13. 12.40 "   A.B.S. reports three red rockets have gone up. This was almost immediately cancelled and ordered not to slacken fire yet.
14. 12.39 "   Bde. Major informed of (12).
15. 12.39 "   Bristol O.P. reports that 5 or 6 red rockets have been sent up from N 8 c 9 7. Enemy also shelling support trenches in front of BRISTOL O.P. and also BOND STREET.
16. 12.41 "   Capt. Moss reports a number of red rockets sent up - apparently from enemy trench.
17. 12.45 "   Bde. Major informed of (15) and (16).
18. 12.55 "   BRISTOL O.P. reports enemy searchlight showing from point 74 (N 14 a 7 3).
19. 12.59 "   Bde. Major informed 18.
20. 1.0 "   Colonel Furse reports that he has not seen any red rockets.
21. 1.2 "   Bde. Major suggests that searchlight should be fired on - replied impossible at present as we do not know definitely where our Infantry are.
22. 1.16 "   BRISTOL O.P. reports that everything on the front is now comparatively calm.
23. 1.17 "   Bde. Major informed (22).
29. 1.14 5   FARM O.P. reports that since 12.15 RUE TILLELOY has been heavily shelled. Four 77 mm. dropped in FARM O.P. Shelling still going on .

25.	1.29 a.m.		R. Battalion reports that everything is quiet on their front & no hostile shelling at all.
26.	1.38	"	Bde. Major informed (25).
27.	1.37	"	Informed by runner from A.B.S. that signal one has been received.
28.	1.38	"	Bde. Major informed (27).
29.	1.43	"	L. Battalion state that they have not heard if Infantry are back or not.
30.	1.44	"	Bde. Major informed (29).
31.	1.42	"	R. Group R.A. asked to continue standing by.
32.	1.56	"	L. Battalion reports that they could not get through wire and are now bringing in wounded.
33.	1.58	"	R. Group informed no need to stand by. Sec. fire (Left Group) 2 min. ordered.
34.	2.10	"	Cease firing to all Batteries.
35.	2.11	"	C.R.A. informed (34).
36.	2.19	"	2/Lieut. Mealing reports Infantry all back.

C/4/6/d
F.5. PROGRAMME

Handwritten notes (left margin):
A — Stop fire on ... points behind line
B — Limmers except on Point 4 of N4 & 96 ?
2 officers at Group HQ, 2 at Div HQ
Inf. ? are sending their officer to B/307 HQ
F were instructed to support line F.3 little hips

A R T I L L E R Y.

ZERO TIMES	INFANTRY.		B/307 Left Group.		Right Group.		Australian.	
0.20	Begin filing out.	0.30	Drills cease.					
0.50	In position.	0.40 – 1.0	Intense on points F.2 & F.4.	0.40 – 1.0	Intense on BIRDCAGE.	0.40 – 1.0	Concentrated on SUGAR LOAF.
0.50	Advance.	0.45 – 0.55	B307 enfilades F.5 front trench.	1.0 – 1.5	Cease fire.		
1.0	Arrive at German trenches.	0.55 – 1.0	B307 enfilades F.5 support trench.	1.5 – 1.20	Lift, and barrage BIRDCAGE.		
		1.0 – 1.40	B307 enfilades ground in rear of F.5 support trench.				
		1.0 – 1.50	Barrage as arranged in rear of F.4 and F.5 and enfilade F.6.				
		1.0 – 1.5	Cease fire on F.2.				
		1.5 – 1.40	Lift, and barrage at F.2.				
1.40	Signal to retire.	2.0 – 2.20	B307 enfilades from F.4 to F.6.				

Time Table.

New Time From	To	Battery	No of guns	Objective	Rate de tir 18pr	4.5	Rate of Fire
Zero	0.30	A/308	4 18pr	J.6.	Ott		Section fire 35" } 5 HE ½ S for frontal fire
		C/308	4 18pr	J.4.	"		" } S for enfilade
		A/307	4 18pr	J.3.	"		"
		D/308.	2 4.5"	J.3.		15	"
		D/307.	2 4.5"	D		15	"
0.40	0.45	D/308.	2 4.5"	F.4. 2guns	40	4	Section fire 2'
				F.2a F.2b. 1 gun each			
		C/308	4 18pr	J.H.	40	4	Section fire 15 secs.
		A/307.	4 18pr	J2a. J.2b.	40		
0.45	0.55	B/307.	4 18pr	Front line J.5	80		"
		C/307.	4 18pr	As before	80		"
		D/308.	4 4.5"	As before		14	Section fire 2'
0.55	1.0	B/307.	4 18pr	Support line J.5	40		Section fire 15 secs
		C/307	4 18pr	[F4, Iz/a e alley from	40		"
		A/307	4 18pr	N13 d.0.3 to N13a. 0.5]	40		" 2'
		D/308	4 4.5"	As before		4	(N.B. on rapid N front point)
				As before			
0.55	1.0	C/308.	4 18pr	N13d 4.4 ½ to N13d. 4½ 2.	40		" 15 secs
				to N13a. 3.15			} HE 2 S for frontal fire
1.0	1.5	B/308	4 18pr	N13c 8 ½. 5 to N19a 9 ½ 9	40		S for enfilade
		D/307	2 4.5"	N13a. 2.15		10	" 30 secs
		D/308.	4 4.5"	N13d 0.2 and N13d 4 ½ 2.		20	" 30 secs
		A/308.	2 18pr	N13a 8.4 to N19a 9 ½ 5 ½	20		15 "
			2 18pr	N19a ½ 6 to N19a. 3.4 ½	20		15 "
		B/307	2 18pr	N19a.½ 6 to N19a. 4.	20		15 "
			2 18pr	N19a. 9 ½ 5 ½ to N19 t. 2&4	20		
				N19.0.5" to N19t 2 ½ 4			

THE TABLE.

Zero Time. From - to.	Battery.	No. of Guns.	Objective.	Rounds. 18pr.	Rounds. 4.5"	Rate of fire.
6-35 / 1-20	A.B.C.D/308. B.D/307. A/307	12-18Prs. 4-18prs. 4-18prs.	As before. As before M.14.c.1.6. to M.14.c.4.3. to M.14.c.7.6.	180 60 60	30 15	Section fire 30 secs. 18-prs. ½ H.E. ½ S. for frontal fire. 1 min. Hows. § for enfilade fire.
	?	4-18prs.	M.14.c.7.6. to M.14.b.3.1. to M.14.a.8.4.	60		
6-50 / 1-20	A.D/308 B/307, D/307.	4-18prs. 4-18prs.	As before. As before M.13.d.1½.5. to M.13.c.9½.2½. to	80 80 80	40 20	Section fire 30 secs. 18prs. 1 min. Hows.
	B/308 ? A/307	4-18prs 4-18pm 4-18prs.	M.13.d.1½.1. M.13.c.5.3. to	90 80		ditto.
1-20 / 2.0 / 1-40	D/307 A.B.D/308 B/307 A/307	1 Gun 4.5" 6-18prs. 4.5" 4-18prs. 4-18prs.	M.13.d.0.2½. As before. M.19.a.9½.9. to M.19.a.4½.4½.	160 80 80	20 40	Section fire 30 secs. 18-prs. 1 min. Hows. ditto.
1-50 / 2.0	B/307		Front line E.6. to F.5. to M.13.d.0.2½.	40		Section fire 1 min. 18prs. Hows. ditto.
1.0 / 6-30 2.0 / 1-30 2.20	2 T.M's. 2 T.M's.		F.2.c. & F.2.b. F.1. to	12 rounds 50 60	" "	As rapidly as possible.

TABLE B.   2/7 Worcesters.

Infantry.	Left Group R.A.	Right Group R.A.	Australian Artillery.	Light Trench Mortars. Right Group.	Light Trench Mortars. Left Group.
10.20 commence filing out.	10.30 Wirecutting etc. drill fire cases.				
10.50 in position ready to advance.	10.40-11 p.m. Intense fire on NICK SALIENT on about N.14.c.4.9.	10.40-11 p.m. Intense fire on BIRDCAGE.	10.40-11 p.m. concentrated fire on SUGARLOAF.	10.40-11.50 8 guns on NICK (from N.13.c. 9½.2 & N.N. of that point).	10.40-11.50.1 gun on NICK. 10.40-1 p.m.)1 gun 1½ (cease fire)CRATER 11p.m.-11.5) 2 guns)on parapet } N.14.a.8. } & 4. m d } to N.E.
	10.45 - 10.55 Enfilade Battery on front trench at point of entry.				11.5-11.40
10.50 Advance.	10.55 - 11p.m. Enfilade Battery on support trench at point of entry.				
11 p.m. arrive at German parapet.	11 p.m.-11.40p.m. Enfilade Battery covers ground in rear of support trench at point of entry.	11 p.m.-11.5 cease fire.			
	11p.m.-11.50p.m. Barrage in rear of point of entry and in rear of NICK SALIENT. Enfilade fire on trench near N.N.19.a. 2h.5.	11.5 - 11.20 lift and barrage BIRDCAGE.			
	11p.m.-11.5 p.m. cease fire about N.14.c.4.9.				
	11.5-11.40 Lift and barrage N.14.c.4.9.				
11.40 signal to withdraw.	12 mid. to 12.20 a.m. Enfilade battery on German fire trench from NICK to N.19.a.2½.5.				

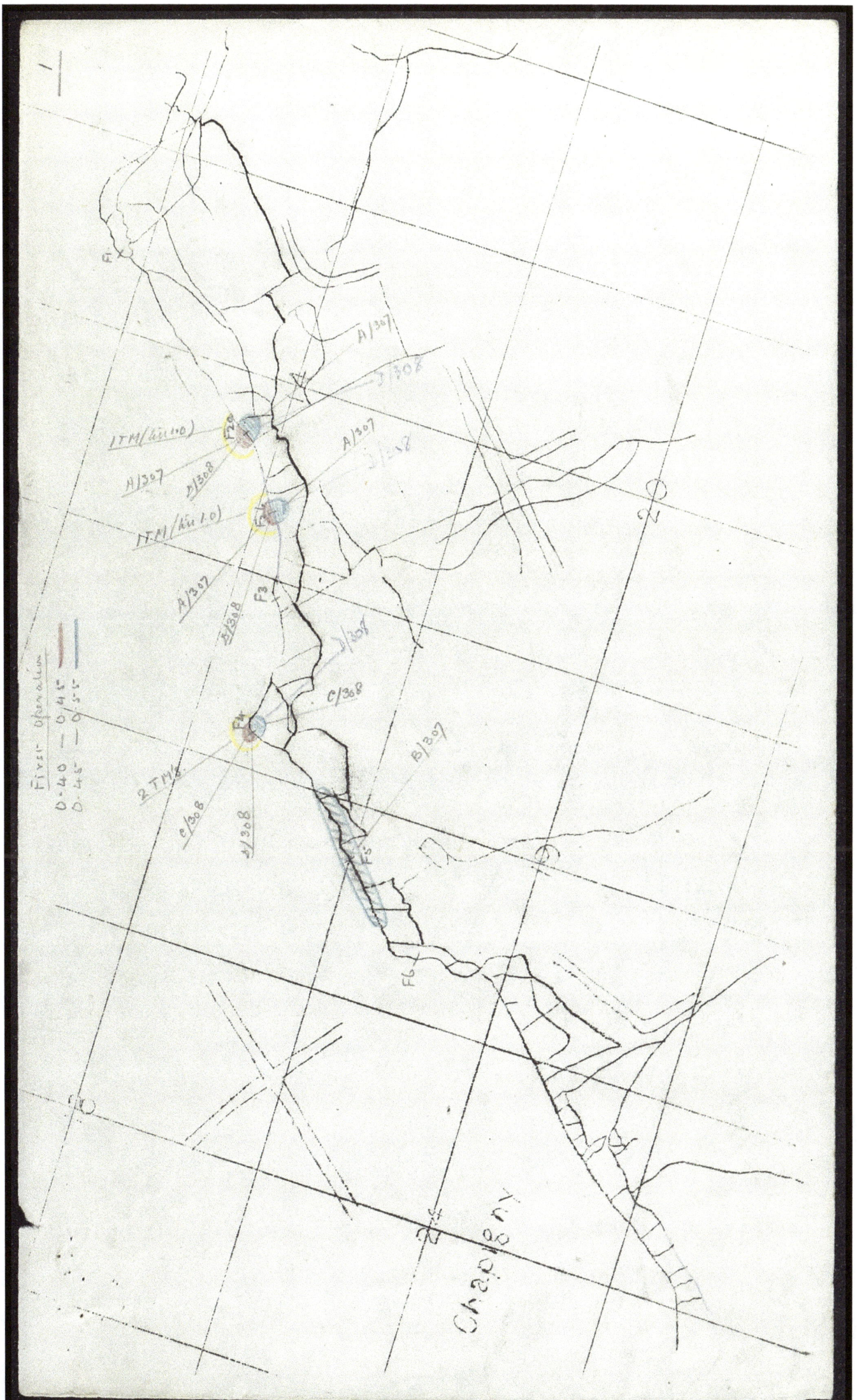

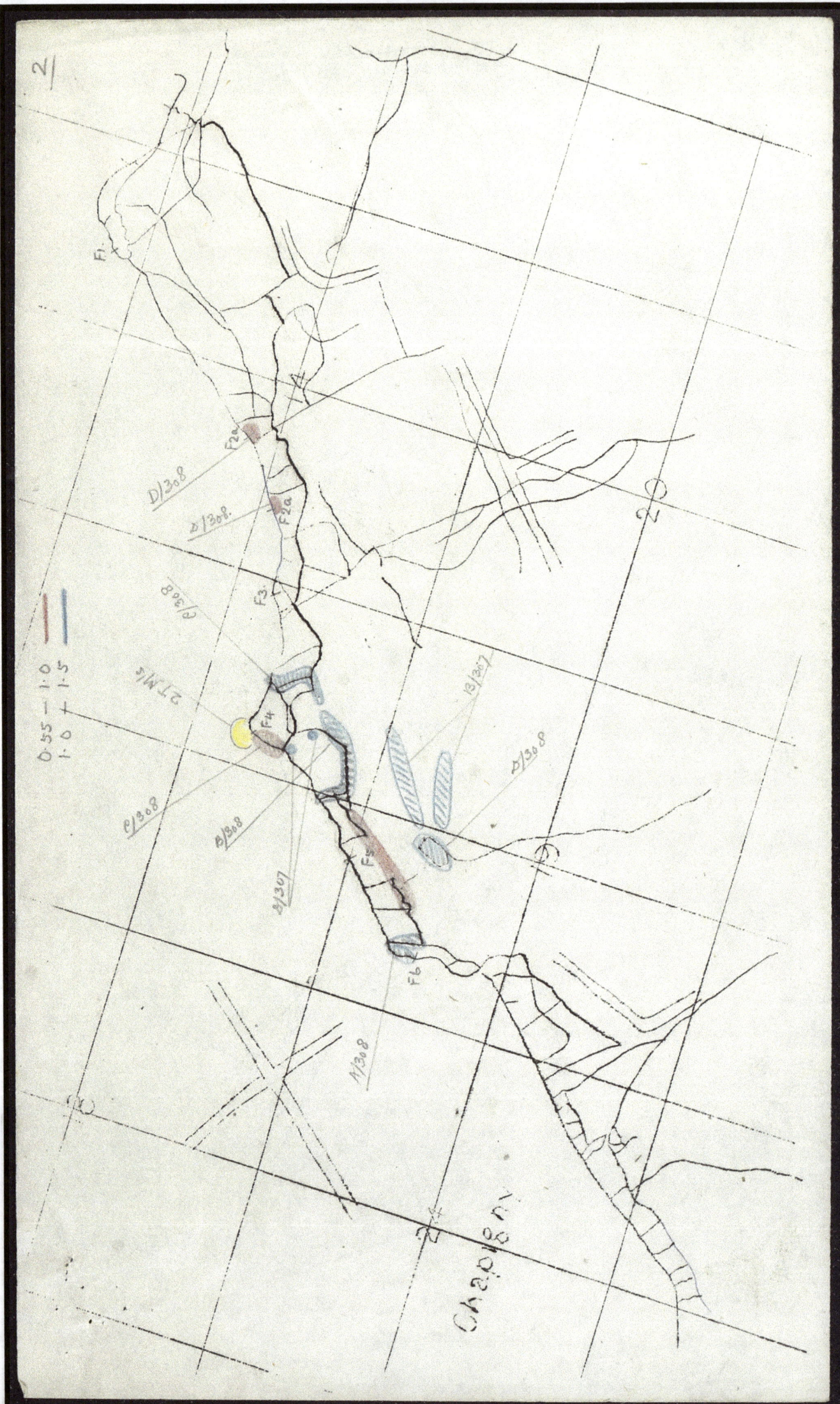

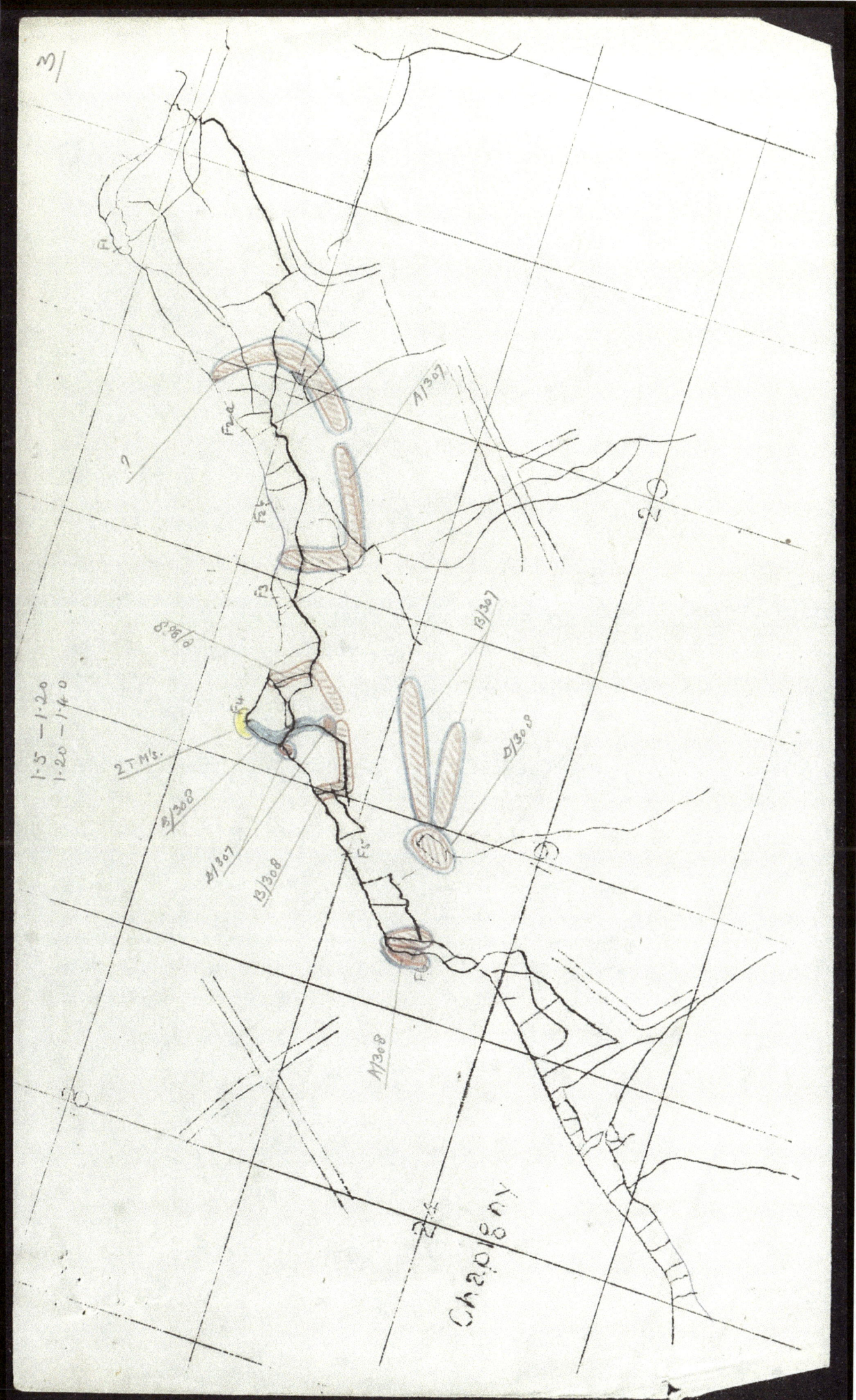

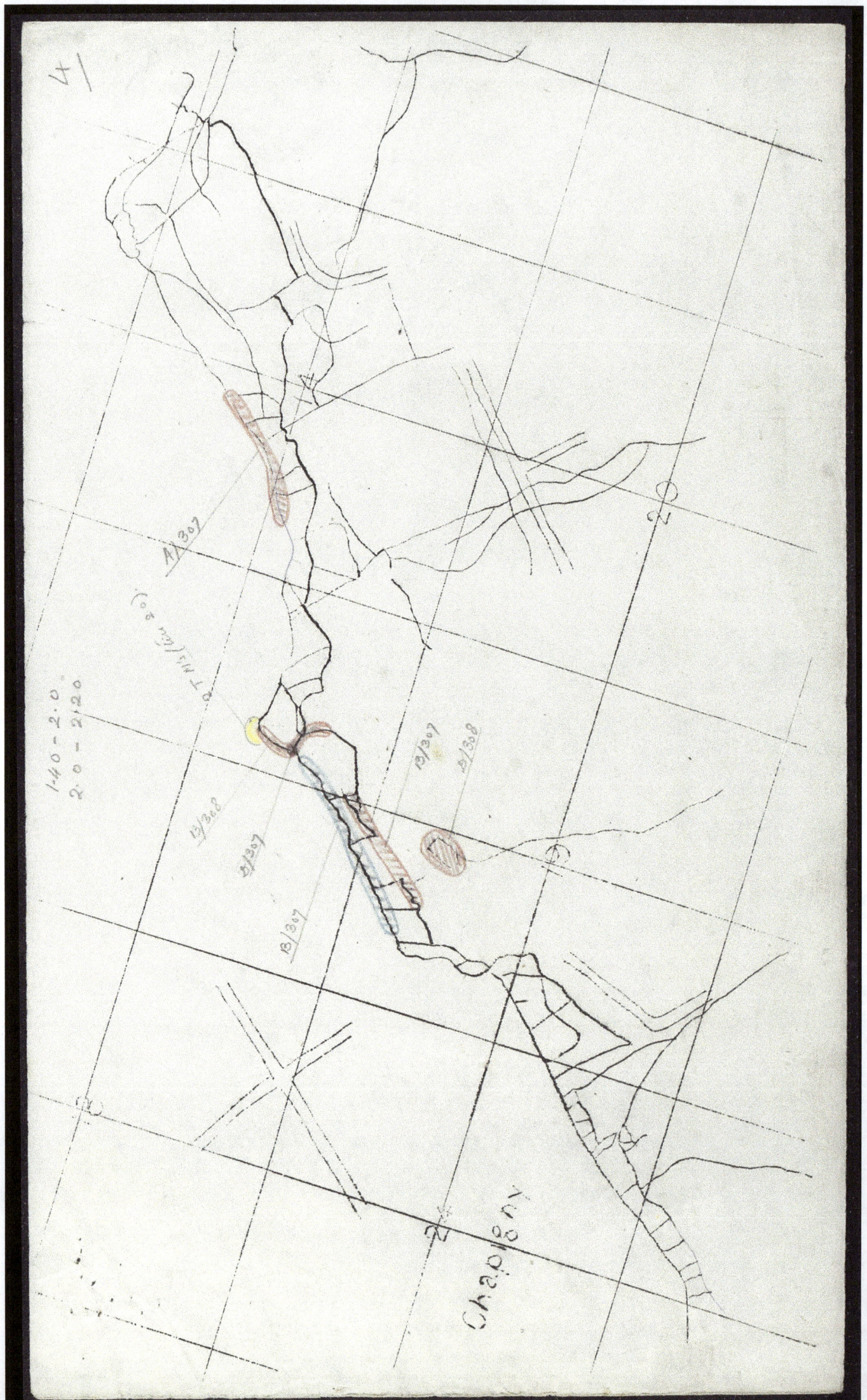

Amendments to Time Table

Phase A — As before
Phase B — As before
Phase C —
  Z
  O
  C/305
  B/305 } As before
  TMS.
  A/306 — Support line N13 d 5.2 to N13 d 8½.4.
  C/306 — Support line N13 d 8½.4 to N14 c 20.55
    Both in addition to support lines already detailed.
  B/RHA — As before } Both Batteries are allotted an
  D/306 — "   "   } additional 150 rounds to those
                      stated in my B/84.

PHASE D   -   As before except that Z/R.H.A. enfilade C.Ts
                at N.20.A.25.75, N.20.a.45.90 to N.20.b.45.10
                and O/RHA enfilade C Ts at N.20.a.45.90;
                N.14.c.55.0 to N.20.b.45.10.

PHASE E   -   As before except that A & C 306 search back to
                front line from N.13.d;3,375 to N 14 .c.2, 6.75
                in addition to the front line already detailed.

PHASE F   -   As before in phase D.

PHASE G   -   As in Phase C.

PHASE H   -   As before in phase D.

PHASE I   -   As in phase E.

PHASE J   -   As before in Phase D.

PHASE K   -   As in Phase C.

PHASE L   -   As before except that A & C 306 remain on
7 - 7.5   the support line at the places detailed
                in place of lifting.

7.5   -   As in Phase D.

NOTE (1)   After 7.00, O & Z Batteries RHA will fire
                50% of their rounds at the head of the
                barrage, distributing the remainder over the
                whole length to N.20.b.45.10.

     (2)   The final barrage at 7.00 will probably be
                kept on all night, special attention being paid
                to the barrages of communication trenches.

     (3)   During the last phase of the bombardment the
                Infantry will deploy in NO MANS LAND and
                assault at 7.00.

D.T.M.O. 8th Div

PROGRAMME FOR T.Ms. Centre Group.

T.Ms Position		Cut wire at	
N12 d 55-90	N 13 d 55 5	20 yds. each side of	N 13 d 5-45 50-45
N13 d 65-95	N 13 d 6.5 9.5	" " "	N 13 d 6.5-5
N 13 d 82-98	N 13 d 82 98	" " "	N 13 d 95-6
N 14 a 0 5	N 14 a 0 5	" " "	N 14 c 1-65
N 14 c 20 30	N 14 A 2 - 33	" " "	N 14 c 35-80
N 14 c 2 30	N 14 A 2 - 3	" " "	N 14 c 45-95

When wire in front line has been cleared at above points, T.Ms have been directed to cut wire from 50 yds. in front of support line during remainder to support line of bombardment, if any time is available.

This programme is only for six T.Ms under Capt. Wallace, 8th Div. T.M.O. He has just informed me that four more guns on his left have been put under his orders, and that he will find out their positions and the points on which they can fire, and will report to me later.

Lt. Col:
Comdg. CENTRE GROUP.

18.7.16.

Apendix "B"

DIARY OF OPERATIONS - 19.7.16.

11.0 a.m.	Zero hour.
11.5 am.	O.C. C305 reported Battery on his right shooting short; passed to B/305.
11.45 am.	Left Battalion reported PICANTIN being shelled with Heavies; passed to Heavies to deal with. Left Battalion reported all troops in position.
12.15 pm.	Reported that H.E; falling short opposite N.14/1.
12.30 pm.	Reported again that enemy shelling PICANTIN and parapet. Also our own H.E. bursting short near N.14/1.
12.35 pm.	Message sent to C/305 to check laying.
1.0 pm.	Laying of C/305 checked and reported O.K.
1.30 pm.	B/305 report whole of O.Ps on RUE TILLELOY are being subjected to a furious bombardment - 5.9 or heavier shells.
2.0 pm/.	RIFLEMAN'S TRENCH by 5.9s forwarded B/305 report to Heavies.
2.27 pm.	Enemy seen retreating to Support Trench opposite N.14
1.58 pm.	Our F.O.O. reports that an aeroplane with British markings identical in pattern with that which was observed flying over our Battery on the 16th is flying up RIFLEMAN'S TRENCH from S.E; to N.W. at a low altitude.
2.20 pm.	Report by Left Group 61st Div. Art. enemy firing a few shrapnel on front line. Stopped shelling support lines. A few shells 77 mm. on BOND STREET, nothing on BURLINGTON ARCADE. Enemy seems to have very few Batteries and to be searching wide with them. Capt. Wallace, "O" Bty. R.H.A. reports wire on his front does not appear to offer serious obstacle, except patch of 20 yards near N.14.c.½.6.6 and 20 yds. near N.14.c.27.
2.35 pm	B/305 being heavily shelled directhit on one gun pit. Remainder carrying on. Report from F.O.O. reports that O.Ps in TILLELOY still being heavily bombarded. Quite out of question to use them. Trying to select TREE O.P. Impossible to make any statement on condition of hostile wire on account of dense smoke. RIFLEMAN'S TRENCH still being heavily shelled.
3.01 pm	D/306 commenced firing on targets in "PHASE C.
3.40 pm.	"O" and "Z" Batteries ordered to turn fire on to support line.
4.0 pm.	Batteries on extreme left of zone ordered to continue on wire with view of widening gaps. Remainder of zone reported practically clear.
4.05 pm.	Report on wire cutting to Divl. H.Q. as follows:- "X9.10.11.12.13 clear. X13 to X14 long grass - impossible to say definitely cut - lots of rounds put into it. X14, 15 clear except for patches. No apparent obstacle to Infantry advance. X16.17, 20 yds. gap now widening. X18, 19, no report" Batteries cutting from 12-16 have turned on to wire in front of support lines.
4.15 pm.	3.51 pm. after barrage was lifted Germans did not increase their fire, but kept up a steady rate on our support and communication trenches. Wire getting very thin. German parapet badly damaged and breached in places. Message from C/305.
4.40 pm.	Shelling by heavy gun at a slow rate not sufficient to constitute a barrage. Message from A/306.
5.00 pm.	Report from C/306 that enemy front line parapet from N.14.c.1.- - N.14.a.8.4. and support line from N.14.c.5.7. - N.14.a.8.1 have been badly damaged and damage is still proceeding. On our lifting, enemy fired slow rate not sufficient to constitute barrage in NO MANS LAND..

(1)

5.35 pm/ 5.40 pm.	Infantry report a lot of shell fire in NO MANS LAND. Ordered O,Z, and D/5 to send Officers to TEA HOUSE, FARM HOUSE, and SNOWDON respectively for night purposes. C/306 report enemy parapet in their sector is a mass of ruins.
6.0 pm.	D/5 report firing appears effective; observation difficult owing to smoke. Hostile retaliation at intervals along TILLELOY with 77 mm., 10.5 cm. and 15 cm. Captain Wallace reported our shells bursting well on hostile trenches.
6.24 pm.	B/305 reports red rocket observed over our lines at 5/53 pm. and a white rocket at 5/55 pm.
6.35 pm.	"O" Bty. reports Germans shelling their own front line. "Z" Bty. report Germans seen firing rifles from west.
6.45 pm.	Infantry seen going over parapet at N.14.c.3.7. Captain Larkwork D/5 Bty. R.H.A. reports particularly heavy hostile barrage machine gun and rifle fire and no infantry movement opposite front N.13/ No hostile shelling on Group front.
7.0 pm.	Message from Bde. Major 61 Div. Art. to effect that some Battery shelling WICK, and must be stopped immediately.
7.10 pm.	Left Battalion report that their attack failed being driven back by Machine Gun fire with heavy casualties. The Battalions on his Left and Right occupied the enemy trenches.
7.30 pm.	Slight shelling of LAVENTIE reported.
7.45 pm.	"O" Bty. reported ammunition in dump down to 50 rds. a gun over their drawing-up point. "Z" Bty. over 100 rds. a gun. "D/5" Bty. 10 rds. a gun over wagon establishment. "A/306" reports hostile shelling between N.14.c/h.6 - N.14;c.3.4. Rate of fire halved for all Batteries, 18 prs one round per gun per 2 minutes. 4.5" Hows. 1 round per gun per 4 minutes. "O" and "Z" Batteries ordered to turn on to front line parapet between WICK and N.13.d.9.6., also sections of A/306 and C/306. "Z" Battery reports that he can see nothing of our Infantry and can see Germans in their front line.
8.0 pm.	D/5 Bty. report rather more hostile fire during last hour, but not heavy. Practically no machine gun or rifle fire.
8.10 pm.	A/306 reporxted nothing seen of Infantry advance; very little hostile shelling except in rear of hostile trenches.
8.30 pm.	Information received from Infantry that except for a party in the German trenches about N.14.c.2.7. all other assaulting Infantry back in our trenches. Contemplated further attack cancelled:-
8.35 pm.	Orders issued to Batteries as follows:- "O" Bty. on N.13.d.96/4, N.14.c.2½.2½ - Nxtxxxxxxx. at 1 round per gun per 4 minutes. A306 and C306 1 section each on N.14.c.2½.2½. - N.14.c.8.6. at 1 round per gun per 4 mins. C/305 on N.14.c.5.9½- N.14.c.8.6. at 1 round per gun per 4 mins. The following at one round per gun per 10 minutes. "Z" Battery N.13.d.9.6. WICK A306 1 Sec. N.13.d.9.6 WICK C306 1 Sec. N.13.d.9.6. WICK B/305 N.14.c.5.9½- N.14.a.7. 9½ D/306 Support Line from N.14.c.7.9½ - N.14.a.9.1½ especially C.T; at latter point.

8-45 pm.		Later. Barrage brought back to front line.
		"O" front line from N 13 d 9.6. to N 14 c 4. 8.
		C/305 " " " N 14 c 3.7½ " N 14 a 5.2.0.
		A/306 " " " N 13 d 9. 6 " WICK
		C/306 " " " N 13 d 9. 6 " N 14 a 7½.3½
11-16 "		Cease fire to all guns except to
		"Z" from N 13 d 0. 4 - N 14 c 0. 6.
		C/305 " N 14 c 0. 6.- N 14 a 5½.22.
		4 salvos per hour on enemy's front line at irregular intervals to prevent enemy repairing wire and parapet.
12.16 pm		C/305 ordered to lift fire on to support trench - as patrol (Infantry) was going out.

                                            (sd) W.P.Bedington

                                                  Capt. & Adjt
                                               CENTRE GROUP

12.50 pm 20/7/16.

Apendisc B.

TIME TABLE

Phase	Period From	Period To	Btys.	Objective.	Rate of Fire and Remarks
A	0	0.30	18-prs & T.M's	Registration	
B	2	4	Z	N.13.d.1½.4½ to N.13.d.8½.5½ and support line and wire in rear	1. For wire-cutting front line 10% HE remainder S. For support line 30% HE to be burst immediately in front of support line parapet
			O	N.13.d.8.5½ to N.14.c.2⅔.7⅓ and support line and wire in rear	
			C/305	N.14.c.2.6¾ to N.14.a.5½.½ and support line and wire in rear	
			B/305	N.14.a.5½.½ to N.14.a.8.3¾ and support line and wire in rear	
			T.M's	From N.13.d.1½.4½ to N.14.a.8.3¾ and support line and wire in rear	
C	4	4.25	Z O C/305 B/305 T.M's	as before	2. For bombardment use 30% S burst as low as possible and short of support line to destroy wire
			A/306	Support line N.14.c.2.5½ to N.14.c.5½.7½	
			C/306	Support line N.14.c.5½.7½ to N.14.a.8½.1½	
			D/RHA	N.14.c.4½.6½ N.14.a.7½.½ N.14.c.5½.8 N.14.a.8½.½	
			D/306	1 Gun on M.G.Emplacement at N.19.d.5.4½ [13]	3. The Heavy T.M. ceases firing during all lifts
D.	4.25	4.29	Z/RHA	Enfilade CTs at N.20.a.2½.7½ N.20.a.4½.9 to N20 b 4½ 1	
			O/RHA	Enfilade CTs at N.14.c.5½.0 N20 a 4½ 9 to N.20.b.4½.1	
			C/305	Lift to Barrage from N.14.c.4.1 to N.14.c.8½.5	
			B/305	Lift to Barrage from N.14.c.8½.5 to N.14.d.3.9	
			A/306	Lift to Barrage from N.20.a.6½.4 to N.14.d.1½.0	
			C/306	Lift to Barrage from N.14.d.1½.0 to N.14.d.7½.5½	
			D/RHA	On area N.20.b.½.3; N.20.b.3.6 N.20.b.3½.3½	
			D/306	On area N.20.b.½.3; N.20.b.3½.1 N.20.b.3½.3½	
			T.M's	Stop Firing	
E.	4.29	5.04		As in phase C, except A & C/306 search backwards to front line from N.14.c.2.6¾ to N.14.a.8.3¾	4. On coming back to front and support line from each lift fire will be intense.
F.	5.04	5.09		Lift as in Phase D.	2 rounds shrapnel per gun per min for 2 mins for 18 prs and 4.5"

6719

TIME TABLE (Cont'd)

Phase	Period From	To	Btys.	Objective	Rate of fire and Remarks
G	5.09	5.29		As in Phase C	5. Heavy T.M. ceases at 7.0
H	5.29	5.36		Lift as in Phase D	6. Rates of fire, with the exception mentioned in 4 above will not exceed 1 rd per gun per min for 18-pr and 1 round per gun per 2 mins for 4.5"
I	5.36	6.21		As in Phase E	
J.	6.21	6.31		Lift as in Phase D	
K.	6.31	7.0		As in Phase C	
L.	7.0			Lift and remain on Barrage Lines. T.M's as before ceasing fire	7. T.M's to fire as fast as possible

16/17th 7/16.

Secret — 16th May 1916

To O.C. —

Herewith programme showing details of Arty Fire starting from O Zero time. Please acknowledge saying whether the programme is understood in all details.

Lt Col
Comdg Centre Group

Vol 4

CONFIDENTIAL

WAR DIARY.

308 A/t Bae

Aug 1st - Aug 31st 1916

VOLUME 4

Army Form C. 2118.

WAR DIARY
or
INTELLIGENCE SUMMARY.
(Erase heading not required.)

CONFIDENTIAL

WAR DIARY.
OF
308th Bde. R.F.A.

From 1st Aug 1916 to 31st Aug 1916.

(VOLUME IIII)

Army Form C. 2118.

308 Bde R.F.A.

WAR DIARY
INTELLIGENCE SUMMARY.
(Erase heading not required.)

Instructions regarding War Diaries and Intelligence Summaries are contained in F. S. Regs., Part II. and the Staff Manual respectively. Title pages will be prepared in manuscript.

Place	Date	Hour	Summary of Events and Information	Remarks and references to Appendices
In the field	Aug 1st		The situation is generally quiet. The enemy shelling the communication trenches and RUE TILLELOY actively. It is reported that quite a number of enemy shells are fully "dud".	
	Aug 2nd		B. Battery carried out registration in conjunction with aeroplane with good results. Twelve men posted from the Brigade to D.A.C. and attached to French Mortars.	
	Aug 3rd		Firing carried out on Trent Line and Back Areas. Very little retaliation by the Enemy.	
	Aug 4th		L.M.B. artillery activity on either side.	
	Aug 5th		The enemy was very busy with his observation balloons, no less than 13 being sent up during the day. An enemy battery at T.2.b.44 was apparently much damaged by one of our heavy batteries.	
	6th		There was no special activity on either side. Our batteries did successful work on the TRAMWAY JUNCTION with the assistance of aeroplane. The enemy made use of a small searchlight to sweep our trenches.	

WAR DIARY   308 Bde RFA   Army Form C. 2118.

INTELLIGENCE SUMMARY.
(Erase heading not required.)

Place	Date	Hour	Summary of Events and Information	Remarks and references to Appendices
In the field	Aug 7th		There was a little hostile fire on RUETILLELOY and our aerodrome. During the night our guns shared the withdrawal of a raiding party which returned with only one casualty having completed their object. A great number of "flicits" were fired by the enemy today. 23 being observed from our O.P.	
	8th		At 3.30 a.m. the enemy suddenly opened fire on our trenches with Artillery and TM's. Soon after three mines were blown at M 30 c 24. Flying in 8 of our dogs the enemy attempted to raid our trenches under cover of machine gun fire, but were repulsed leaving some dead. The artillery opened fire on their support lines. The remainder of the day passed quietly.	
	9th		The enemy put over the normal number of shells on our support line and RUETILLELOY. The Battery BRISTOL O.P. also being shelled but no damage was done under their fire 3 direct hits being observed.	
	10th		Very little activity on either side.	

Army Form C. 2118.

WAR DIARY
or
INTELLIGENCE SUMMARY.
(Erase heading not required.)

3ᵒᶠ Bde R.F.A.

Place	Date	Hour	Summary of Events and Information	Remarks and references to Appendices
In the field	11 Aug		Firing on the Enemy front line and back areas was carried out by our artillery.	
	12		2/Lt B.S. GORTON started to hospital.	
	13		We bombarded the Enemy front and support line system with trench mortars supported by field guns. The firing was very effective doing a considerable amount of damage and causing the enemy to retaliate rather heavily.	
	14		A defensive mine was fired during the afternoon in he MOATED GRANGE SECTION. Our French mortars were again active.	
	15		The usual amount of artillery fire on both sides.	
	16		2/Lt W.B. BOON attached from C/308 Bde to Heavy Trench howitzers. The Enemy sent up from pigeons which crossed our line.	
	17 18 19		Enemy line was little and active activity. The special activity he continued a programme of firing on enemy front & support line system.	

WAR DIARY
of
INTELLIGENCE SUMMARY.

(Erase heading not required.)

Army Form C. 2118.

3rd Bde. R.F.A.

Place	Date	Hour	Summary of Events and Information	Remarks and references to Appendices
In the field	Aug 19th		After a preliminary bombardment by our artillery a raiding party left our trenches on arriving at the German parapet it was found to be fully manned. Some bombs were exchanged and the party withdrew to our lines with one or two casualties. A second raiding party later entered the enemy trench, killed a number of the enemy and withdrew losing in all 6 officers and 6 men killed. The raid was also covered by the fire of our artillery.	
	20th			
	21st 22nd 23rd		No abnormal activity on the front. The enemy shelled the RUE TILLELOY and O.P's. Several hits obtained on the CONVENT O.P. — Some damage being done to the protecting wall in front of the O.P. Our Artillery co-operated with the 31st D in Art in support of raid by 92nd Inf. Bde.	
	24th		The usual shelling of the enemy trenches continued this day	

Army Form C. 2118.

WAR DIARY
or
INTELLIGENCE SUMMARY.
(Erase heading not required.)

Place	Date	Hour	Summary of Events and Information	Remarks and references to Appendices
In the field	Aug 25		No especial activity on the front	
	26th			
	27			
	28		2/Lt B.S. Gordon returned to duty. Our artillery fired heavily on enemy wire, front and support line trenches. Much material damage was done. Very little retaliation by the enemy in reply to our fire. Our artillery also bombarded the SUGAR LOAF and the WICK in cooperation with the 5th Australian Divisional Artillery.	
	29			
	30		Wire cutting has been further proceeded with and good results obtained. The naval firing on coast areas was carried out.	
	31st		No abnormal activity on either side	

W. Dunn Lt Col
Cmdg 2/8th Bn. Pl Fus.

Vol 5

CONFIDENTIAL

WAR DIARY

308th ART BDE

Sept 1 – 30. 1916

VOL V

Army Form C. 2118.

WAR DIARY
or
INTELLIGENCE SUMMARY.
(Erase heading not required.)

CONFIDENTIAL

WAR DIARY
OF
308 Bde R.F.A.

FROM 1st SEPT 1916 to 30th SEPT 1916

(VOLUME IV)

WAR DIARY
INTELLIGENCE SUMMARY
(Erase heading not required.)

Army Form C. 2118.

308 Bde. R.F.A.

Place	Date	Hour	Summary of Events and Information	Remarks and references to Appendices
	1916			
LAVENTIE	Sept 1st	6 pm	1st. Combined shoot of 1 Sept. 4.5 How Artillery, M.T.M's, L.T.M's and rifle grenades on enemy trenches. M 24 d 7/4, 3 3/4 to M 24 d 9.1 3/4 also on Trench from M 24 d 4/1/2 and on F.L. M 24 d 5.1 M 24 d 7. 3/3/2. Considerable damage done to trenches. Enemy MINNENWERFER opened fire on our trenches. He replied with 1.18 pr. 4.1. 4.5 How Battery, causing a tremendous explosion exactly at the spot the flash appeared to come from. The MINNENWERFER has not since fired from this spot & was probably knocked out.	
			2. Several horse shoes and spots.	
	2nd		C/308 Bde takes two guns into forward wire cutting position to cut wire. B/308 cut wire from their present position. M.T.M.s cut wire morning and afternoon.	
	3rd		3. The 182 Infantry Bde relieve 184 Infantry Bde. Lt Col E. M¹ I was taken over command of Right Group relieving Lt Col F. Hidden at 12 noon	
	4th		4. Major Austin of A/308 is struck off the strength of the Bde from 24/8/16	

Army Form C. 2118.

308 Bde R.F.A.

WAR DIARY
INTELLIGENCE SUMMARY.
(Erase heading not required.)

Place	Date	Hour	Summary of Events and Information	Remarks and references to Appendices
	4th		Capt H P Smith transferred to unit from C/306 Bde as from 23/8/16. 2 Lt W B Browne posted to C/306 A.C. as from 26/8/16. 2 Lt M Gordon posted to M.T.M. as from 1/9/16. M.T.M.'s covered by one 18pr Battery fired for 20 minutes on enemy wire doing good work. A large percentage of enemy shells were reported to be blind.	
	5th		6 in M.T.M.'s fired 33 rounds, knocking parapet at N.14.a.6.2/2. The enemy H.T.M. opened fire but was silenced after firing 6 rounds. Four of our Batteries and the H.T.M.'s fired on enemy front line and C.T.'s, in conjunction with the 5th Australian Div Art.	
	6th		6 in M.T.M.'s fired on enemy wire & parapet, doing much damage. A raid was carried out by the 2/8th Warwicks and another by the 2/6th Warwicks. Artillery operations are appended in appendix A.	
	7th		Hostile MINENWERFER's firing from N.14.d.35.15 and N.19.c.17.5.100 were silenced by our artillery. Communication Trenches were fired on at irregular intervals.	

WAR DIARY
INTELLIGENCE SUMMARY

308th Bde. R.F.A. Army Form C. 2118.

Place	Date	Hour	Summary of Events and Information	Remarks and references to Appendices
LAVANTIE	8th Sept.		Our artillery made a small bombardment on the front line to the EAST of THE WICK. The trenches were considerably damaged & co-operated with the Australian Artillery in the evening, from of our Batteries bombarding the Sugar SUGAR LOAF. Two of our batteries also bombarded the enemy trenches NORTH of the BIRDCAGE at a quick rate of fire for 3 minutes. This was in conjunction with the Right Group. Very slight retaliation was given by the enemy.	
	9th		Medium trench mortars fired on enemy saps, doing considerable damage. They were covered by fire of three 18in Batteries. A raid was carried out by the 2/6 Warwicks, a barrage being established by two 18pr Batteries. A Bangalore torpedo was fired at a point away from the point of entry to divert the enemy's attention. Very slight hostile retaliation was given. Shots were fired during the night at irregular intervals on new work at N.14.c.7.4 to prevent progress being made with this work.	

Army Form C. 2118.

308 Bde R.F.A.

WAR DIARY
INTELLIGENCE SUMMARY.
(Erase heading not required.)

Place	Date	Hour	Summary of Events and Information	Remarks and references to Appendices
LAVENTIE	16th Sept.		Working parties and fatigues moving along RUE DELVAL were fired upon and dispersed. Italian T.M's bombarded enemy front line from 3.15 h. 6.30. The enemy parapet was totally destroyed at junction of RED RIVER's F.t. Enemy retaliated with 6 rounds from their Minenwerfer which was silenced by our artillery. The Minenwerfer also opened fire at 3.20 a.m. firing 6 rounds. This was silenced by fire from three of our Batteries. A time Co operation was arranged with the T.M's by which the T.M. was fired immediately before the burst of the 18/p shell. The shell arrived in preventing the observation of the T.M. bd. by the enemy in the front line. Only slight retaliation with 77 m.m. on line.	
			6 in Heavy artillery shelled the Minenwerfer emplacement at N.14.B. 3½. 1½ at 5.54 p.m. On the fall of the first shell, 4 men were seen to run away from Hd.	

WAR DIARY or INTELLIGENCE SUMMARY

Army Form C. 2118.

3ᵒ Bde RFA

Place	Date	Hour	Summary of Events and Information	Remarks and references to Appendices
LAVENTIE	11ᵗʰ	5pm	Tulin Trench covered by fire of 18pr Batteries did considerable damage to enemy firing line between N14.c.8.9 and N14.c.1½.6½.	
	12ᵗʰ		M.mmenwerfer opened fire on N14.1. This was engaged by our 18pr and silenced. Our Heavy Artillery fired 20 rounds at HTM emplacement at N14.b.35.15. Smoke of these shots appeared to be direct hits and the HTM has not fired since. It has been reported that there appear to be no 5.9 Batteries on this front at the present time. The enemy retaliation is not vigorous and consists mostly of 77m from 8.9.16.	
	13ᵗʰ		2ⁿᵈ S.F. EMPSON is appointed Adjutant to B/305 13th Bde RFA with effect from 8.9.16.	
			1341 Bʳ Jones P.T. evacuated to England 5/9/16.	
			1984 F.M Sgt Morris " " " 3/9/16.	
			The building of additional Battery positions is being carried on and as soon as possible one gun taken into each position registered.	

WAR DIARY
or
INTELLIGENCE SUMMARY.
(Erase heading not required.)

Army Form C. 2118.

3rd Bde R.F.A.

Place	Date	Hour	Summary of Events and Information	Remarks and references to Appendices
LAVENTIE.	14th Sept.		A combined shoot by our M.T.M's and Howitzer battery did much damage to enemy parapet at N.14.a.9.6. Several working parties were fired on and dispersed during the day, the enemy seeming to be particularly active in doing repair work.	
	15th		Further activity of our M.T.M's did considerable damage to enemy trench, much timber and earth was thrown up. A number of 77mm shells fired into this area during the day are reported blind.	
	16th		A combined shoot of M.T.M's and 6" Howitzer took place on enemy staff at N.13.d.20.45. Much damage resulted, the enemy parapet was much knocked about and direct hits obtained. The 6. Div Art takes over positions in NEUVE CHAPELLE sector from 31st Div Art. The 307 Brigade took over this new sector. Three Groups were formed. Lt Col KOEBEL commanding the RIGHT GROUP. O Col WILLIX the CENTRE Group & Lt Col FURSE the LEFT Group.	

WAR DIARY
INTELLIGENCE SUMMARY.
(Erase heading not required.)

Army Form C. 2118.

Place	Date	Hour	Summary of Events and Information	Remarks and references to Appendices
LAVENTIE	16th Sept.		The 61st Div. Art. is re-organised Batteries now being 6 Gun Batteries instead of 4 Gun Batteries. In this Brigade one Section (Right) of C.308 was transferred to A.308. The left section of C.308 was transferred to B.308. Major H.D. DAY assumed command of A.308. Nominal roll of Officers appended. The LEFT Group was composed of three 18 pdr Batteries (A.308, B.308 and B.308) and one Howitzer B.308, taking the zone from the NORTH of the SUGARLOAF to MY 4 28.5. 2 Lt K.W. MEALING posted to B.308. 2 Lt H.D. SCOTT posted to 308 Bde Hqrs as Orderly Officer.	
	17th		New Sections of A.308 and B.308 and B.308 are in their positions and B.306 has taken up its new position and reported to zone. A rifle pit was destroyed by our artillery and the trench mortars did much damage to a double mine shaft. Hostile fire has decreased very considerably and very slight retaliation or none at all is given for our fire	

WAR DIARY

INTELLIGENCE SUMMARY.

(Erase heading not required.)

3rd Bde R.F.A. Army Form C. 2118.

Place	Date	Hour	Summary of Events and Information	Remarks and references to Appendices
LAVENTIE	18 Sept		Gun M.T.M. again damaged the Emmy F.L. trench. Practically no artillery activity on the front.	
	19	-	A considerable about of M.T.M.s and on 18pr Battery on front and support lines was successful in damaging enemy works. Reinforcements arrived, 11 details posted to Batteries of the Brigade.	
	20	*	Snipers shot at working parties during the night. Was fired on new trench N.14 c/7.4. Much work has been done here recently and it is thought necessary to stop or hinder the work.	
	21st 22nd 23rd	}	Continued shoots of M.T.M.s & covered by 18pr.	
			More aerial activity then usual, three machines were on our line during the day.	
	24		Gun Howitzer Battery obtained direct hits on M.G.E. at N.19 a 35.40. This emplacement in two shows for damage to be done by a 4.5" How.	

Army Form C. 2118.

3 of B.d. R.F.A

WAR DIARY
or
INTELLIGENCE SUMMARY.
(Erase heading not required.)

Instructions regarding War Diaries and Intelligence Summaries are contained in F. S. Regs., Part II. and the Staff Manual respectively. Title pages will be prepared in manuscript.

Place	Date	Hour	Summary of Events and Information	Remarks and references to Appendices
LAVENTIE	25th Sept.			
	26th		Continued shoots by MTMs & 18 prs. Nothing else of interest.	
	27th			
	28th		Hostile Minenwerfer silenced by our artillery. This opened fire in reply to our MTMs, which did considerable damage.	
	29th		Hostile minenwerfer again opened fire and was silenced after firing two rounds. Slightly more hostile fire reported.	
	30th		Our 14 T Ms and MTMs combined in a shoot with 2.18 pdr Battery covering them. The HTM fired 7 rounds 5 of which were effective. Of the other two, one was very short and one a premature, bursting in No Man's Land. Enemy trench was very much damaged. Hostile artillery appear to be checking their registration during the day, making it appear that a relief had taken place.	

Manshire
Col. Rd.
3 of B.d R.F.A

VERY SECRET   B 77   Copy No. 11
                                6/9/16.

Ref. Bde. Trench Map
Area K.
INSTRUCTIONS FOR ENTERPRISE NIGHT OF
6/7th INST. Sept 1916.

1. In view of the important operations in progress in the South, it is of the utmost importance to obtain identifications at the present time. The 182nd Inf. Bde. are therefore raiding the enemy's trenches tonight.

2. The 2/8th Warwicks. will raid the USGAR LOAF at N.8.d.20.15. Artillery will fire as shown in Table 1.

3. The 2/6th Warwicks. will raid enemy's trenches at N.19.a.3.5. using Bangalore Torpedoes to cut the wire. Artillery will fire as in Table 2, noting instructions regarding time when fire is to be opened.

4. 2/Lieut. Wood, A/307, will act as forward control Officer with L.B.
2/Lieut. Roberts will act as forward control Officer with R.B. Both report at respective Battn. Headquarters at 8 p.m.

5. Half an hour after firing has ceased A/308 and C/308 will fire 4 salvos at irregular intervals on C.T's at least 100 yards from the point of entry of raiding party.

6. Watches will be synchronised at 7 p.m. tonight.

7. Reports during operations and immediately afterwards will be sent to Group Headquarters.

8. Acknowledge.

                      Sidney F. Empson
                      Lt & Adj Left Group.

Issued at

Copy No.1   61 Div. Art.   Copy No.6   B/308
    No.2   182 Inf Bde.   No.7   C/308
    No.3   A/307   No.8   D/308
    No.4   B/307   No.9   D.T.M.O.
    No.5   A/308   No.10 File
                                    No.11 War Diary.

TABLE 1.

TIME	Batteries	Objective	Rounds	Rate of Fire
10.53 - 11.13	A/307) C/308) B/307) T/M's)	As from 4.0 - 4.30 A/307, C/308. Bombard also from N.8.d.20.15 to N.8.d.35.20. with Ax. Ammunition. T.M's concentrate on point N.8.d.20.15 cutting wire at this point if a gap there has not been made already until 11.3 pm. then lift to Junction of C.T. and tramway lines at N.14.d.20.75.	A/307) 30 rds. A. C/308) 30 rds. Ax. B/307- 80 rds. A. T.M's as many as possible.	Section fire 40 secs. Section fire 30 secs.
11.13 - 11.18.	Cease fire			
11.18 - 11.48	A/307 (1 section) C/308 (1 gun) (3 guns) B/307	N.8.d.40.30. to N.8.d.65.00 N.14.b.0.8. to N.14.b.25.75. N.14.b.0.8. to N.14.a.60.15. N.8.d.55.25 to N.14.b.25.75.	30 rounds 30 rounds 60 rounds 60 rounds.	Section fire 1 min. Gun fire 1 min. Section and gun fire 1 min. Section fire 1 min.

Batteris shooting on front line are to shorten their range 50 x short of the enemy's parapet.

----

for Lieut-Colonel Comandg.
LEFT GROUP R.A.

TABLE 2.
----

2 Green Rockets will be the signal that one Bangalore Torpedo has been fired. They should be fired about 11.5 p.m. Zero time will be taken fom the time the Bangalore Torpedo has been fired.

TIME	Battery	Objective	Rounds	Rate of Fire.
0.20 - 0.50	B/308 (1 gun)	N.19.a.4.7. to N.19.a.55.55	15)	Gun fire 2 mins.
	(3 guns)	N.19.a.4.7. to N.13.c.8.1	45)	and Section Fire 1 min.
	A/308 (1 gun)	N.19.a.30.25 to N.19.a.40.25	15)	
	(3 guns)	N.19.a.30.25 to N;19.c.15.85	45)	
	D/308 (1 gun).	N.19.a.35.05.	12	Gun fire 2½mins.
	(1 gun)	N.19.a; 45.10.	12	ditto.
	(1 gun)	N.19.a.80.45	12.	ditto.
	(1 gun)	N.19.a.65.65	12	ditto

Batteris shooting on front line are to shorten their range to 50x short of the enemy"'s parapet.

for Lieut-Colonel comndg.
LEFT GROUP.

6/9/16

OPERATIONS - 6/7th Septr.1916.

10.53 pm.	Our Batteries opened fire on SUGAR LOAF as per programme.
11.8 "	Enemy retaliation on PICANTIN and Support Trenches at N.8.1 and 4/2"s and 77 mm. Reported by A/307.
11.9 "	The H.T.M. reported firing from N.14.b.35.15. Two of our guns put on to this. One C/308 and one B/307.
11.15 "	A/307 reports retaliation on N.8.2.
11.25 "	B/307 reports Minnenwerfer has not fired again so they are not carrying on at that point. C/308 were still kept on this.
11.29 "	Infantry report rate of fire too slow. A/307 and C/308 told to increase rate of fire to section fire 15 seconds.
11.40 "	A/307 report enemy artillery very quiet so we slacken down to original rate of fire.
11.52 "	Cease firing left Sector.
12.0 midnight	Enemy shelling N.8.2 and support trenches with 4.2".
12.5 a.m.	hostile shelling ceased. About 60 rounds came over in all.
12.16 "	Bangalore Torpedo was blown. Green rockets sent up, and all our guns commenced firing as per programme.
12.18 "	Infantry reported to have gone over.
12.24 "	Hostile shelling reported to be NIL.
12.28 "	Right Battalion asked us to increase rate of fire. Rate of fire doubled.
12.30 "	Considerable hostile shelling on N.13.1.
12.31 "	Infantry reported returned and our Forward Officer told to cease firing by the Infantry.
12.32 "	All Batteries ceased fire.

Sidney F. Capson Lt

for Lieut-Colonel comndg.
LEFT GROUP.

APPENDIX B.

NOMINAL ROLL OF OFFICERS 61 Div. Art.
on reorganisation into 6 gun Batteries.

306th Bde.
Lt-Col F.G.Willock
Adjt.Capt. F.H.Hooper.
O/Offr.2/Lt.F.J.Baly.

A/Battery
Captain W.H.Taylor
Captain W.P.Bedington
Lieut. A.H.Hughes.
2/Lieut. F.M.S.Kent.
2/Lt.R.H.W.Maddock

B/Battery.
Captain N.M.Penny
Captain I.T.Rowe
Lieut.J.G.W.Hendrie
Lieut.J.R.A.Evans
2/Lt.P.H.Leach

C Battery
Captain T.M.Duncan
2/Lieut W.H.Unwin
2/Lt. T.R.Page
2/Lt H. Copley
2/Lt N.J. Richards.

D Battery
Major E.S. Harris
Lieut I.S. Hart
2/Lt H.L.Wilson
2/Lt E.S. Bishop
Lieut F.T.Cale

307th Bde
Lt-Col. H.A.Koebel
Adjt. Capt.A.G.Noble.
O/Offr.2/Lt.A.V.McDowell

A/Battery
Major A.O.Bowall
Capt. G.L.Pain
Lieut. A.A.Prentice
2/Lt. T.S.Wood
2/Lt R.V.Caddick

B Battery
Capt. J.R.Barry
Capt. W.G.Poore
Lieut P.L.Z.Lea
2/Lt.P.S.Marshall
2/Lt C.S. Youngs

C Battery
Capt. B.F. Huggins
Capt. H.Lowe
Lieut. A. Watson
Lieut. A.E.S.Barton
2/Lt W.J.Wilkins

D Battery
Major A.A.Torrens
Lieut E.S.L.Ostler
2/Lt I.C.Lyster
2/Lt C.H.Wilkins
2/Lt L.E. Barton

308th Bde.
Lt-Col. E.W.Furse
Adjt.Lieut.S.F.Empson.
O/Offr.2/Lt.M.D.Scott.

A Battery
Major H.D.Day
Capt. G.S. James
Lieut. S.L.Dickinson
2/Lt F.L. Perowne
2/Lt H.G. Boberts

B Battery
Capt. W.C. Caldicott
Capt. H.B.Smith
Lieut. B.H. Smith
Lieut G.H.Smith
2/Lieut W.G.Barnard

D Battery
Captain T.J.MOSS
Lieut V.Macnamara.
2/Lt.K.W.Mealing.
2/Lt.C.S.Callingham.
2/Lt.C.W.Killby.

SURPLUS OFFICERS
Temporarily attached to
Brigade as follows.

306th Bde
2/Lt.F.H.Hole.
2/Lt.E.J.Davis.
2/Lt.N.C.Barnes.
2/Lt.C.B.Chilverd.

307th Bde
Capt.C.K.S.Metford
2/Lt.G.G.Bull.
2/Lt.A.McLean.
2/Lt.R.M.Montgomery.
Lieut.J.C.Fielding.

308th. Bde.
2/Lt.E.Ralli.
2/Lt.J.F.Sutton.
2/Lt.L.C.Godwin.
Lieut.W.G.Clinton.

Captain G.S. Stockman A/306 not included in
above, will be posted to Command No.3 Section
D.A.C. where a vacancy exists.

Staff Captain R.A.
61st Division.

R.A. H.Q.
16/9/16

Vol 6

CONFIDENTIAL

WAR DIARY

308 ART BDE

Oct. 1 - 31 - 1946

VOL 6

Army Form C. 2118.

WAR DIARY
INTELLIGENCE SUMMARY.
(Erase heading not required.)

CONFIDENTIAL

WAR DIARY
OF
308 Bde R.F.A.

From 1st Oct 1916 to 31st Oct 1916

(VOLUME VI)

WAR DIARY or INTELLIGENCE SUMMARY.

Army Form C. 2118.

308 Bde RFA

Place	Date	Hour	Summary of Events and Information	Remarks and references to Appendices
LAVENTIE	1916 Oct 1st		At 10 a.m. an Albatros was observed flying at our driven back by our A.A. guns. A combined shoot by HTMs – MTMs and 18prs was very successful in one of ever club fired by the HTMs were effective doing much damage. During the night the 2/7th Warwicks carried out a raid on the enemy trenches at N19a 62.92. Wire was cut at the front by our MTMs and fourful trench Machine gun emplacements on either side of point of entry were effectively dealt with by our MTMs. A barrage was established by our Artillery as in operation orders in appendix A. The raid was a success; being carried out exactly to time, the party after occupying the trenches for 10 minutes entering dug outs and killing a considerable number of Germans and bringing in one wounded prisoner. There were no casualties to the raiding party.	

B.122. 1/10/16

VERY SECRET

Copy No.... 6....
1/10/16.

Ref: Bde. Trench Map
Area K.

INSTRUCTIONS FOR ENTERPRISE NIGHT OF 1/2nd OCTOBER 1916.

1. A raid will be carried out by the 182nd Infantry Brigade with the object of securing identifications and inflicting losses on the enemy; and to blow up any mine shafts in the vicinity.

2. The 2/7th Warwicks. will raid the enemy trench at N.19.a.62.92.

3. Artillery will fire as shown in Table "A".

4. Lieut. Macnamara, D/308 will act as forward control officer.

5. Watches will be synchronised by Group Hdqrs. at 7.30 pm.

6. X. Reports during operations and immediately afterwards, will be sent to Group H.Q.

7. ACKNOWLEDGE.

Sidney Hopson

Lieut & Adjutant,
LEFT GROUP.

Issued at ....

Copy No. 1 61 Div.Art.
" " 2 182 Inf.Bde.
" " 3 B/308
" " 4 D.T.M.O.
" " 5 File
" " War Diary.

VERY SECRET B.

Reference Group Order B.122 of 1/10/16, the Zero Time is 9 pm.

Sidney Thompson

Lieut & Adjutant;
LEFT GROUP.

1.10.16.

Zero Time..............

TIME TABLE "A".

Time From.	To.	Battery.	No. of Guns.	Objective.	Rounds. 18 pdrs.	Rounds. Ax	Rate of fire.
0.10	0.32	B/308	2 guns	N.19.a.5.50. 7.75 (Junction of C.T. and front line)	48) 40) 96)		First 4 minutes Sec. Fire 5" Next 10 minutes Sec. Fire 15" Last 8 minutes Sec. Fire 5"
"	"	B/308	2 guns	N.13.c.8.25. 0.25. (Junction of C.T. and front line.)	48) 40) 96)		
0.00	0.10	M.T.M.	2 guns	N.19.a.6.25. 9.25. (Junction of C.T. and front line "P of E)	20)		As fast as possible.
			1 gun	M.G.E. (N.13.c.800.025 = 65x North of P of E.		10)	
			1 gun	M.G.E. (N.19.a.600.875. = 40x South of P of E.		10)	
0.00	0.10	L.T.M.	2 guns)	N.19.a.750.950. Sweep 50x Left to extreme range Sweep 50x			As fast as possible.
0.10	0.14	do.	2 guns)				
0.00	0.10	do.	2 guns)	N.19.a.575.850. Sweep 50x Left to extreme range. Sweep 50x			
0.10	0.14	do.	2 guns)				
0.00	0.32	do.	1 gun.	N.19.a.400.700.			Slow rate of fire.
0.00	0.32	do.	1 gun.	N.13.d.000.325.			

COPY

REPORT ON RAID CARRIED OUT BY 2/7TH WARWICKS
on the night of 1st Octr.1916.

At 8.30 pm. the raiding party left our trenches and hid in No Man's Land, evidently without being seen by the enemy, as no firing occured.

At 9.0 pm. according to programme, our Light and Medium Trench Mortars opened a very fast rate of fire along the enemy's front in the vicinity of the "point of entry". This fire lasted for 10 minutes, and appeared to be very accurate - no rounds were observed to fall short.

At 9.10 pm. this fire lifted, and the raiding party advanced without any opposition in any way, and entered the enemy's trenches, bombed dugouts, and captured one prisoner. One large dugout was blown up by the Australian miner who accompanied the party.

During the time the raiders were in the enemy's trenches, two machine guns commenced firing from about N.13.c.85.10. One of these guns traversed our parapet and the other swept No Man's Land. This firing only lasted for a few seconds as the guns were evidently silenced by the fire of our Batteries.

The raiding party remained in the enemy trenches about 12 minutes. All returned to our lines without a casualty, after ascertaining that everything was correct. I gave the order to "Cease Fire" and remained in front line till 10 pm.

The fire of our Batteries and Trench Mortars was splendid.

The enemy's reply was most feeble. He only fired 10 rounds of 4.2" Hows. near our Support Line. This fire appeared to come from the direction of FROMELLES and came after the raid was over. During the raid, the enemy sent up 4 red bouquet rockets, which appeared to come from his Support Line.

The raid was well planned and carried out, and the success appeared to be largely due to the accurate and overwhelming fire of our Trench Mortars.

(Sd.) V.MACNAMARA   Lieut.
Liaison Officer,
D/308 Bty.

1st Octr.1916.

WAR DIARY
INTELLIGENCE SUMMARY.
(Erase heading not required.)

Army Form C. 2118.

308 Bde R.F.A.

Place	Date	Hour	Summary of Events and Information	Remarks and references to Appendices
LAVENTIE	1916 Sept 2nd		Lt Col F H Dobson to take temporary command of 308 Bde R.F.A. and Left Group from 26th Sept 1916. The N.T.M.s made good shooting on the WICK and the M.T.M.s attempted did good during the mine shafts attached to the WEST of the WICK. Increased activity of the hostile artillery was noticed, and in the enemy a number of 4.2s & 77s were fired to the SOUTH of FAUQUISSART.	
	3rd		M.T.M.s continued their firing on Mine shafts. Enemy retaliated with a few rounds from their M.T.M.s	
	4th		The artillery dispersed several working parties during the day. Fire Reinforcements were taken on the strength of the Brigade from No. 1 Territorial Base Depot. M.T.M.s fired on wire and also on parapet and sap at N.14.c.3.00.725. Two good gaps in the wire and much damage the enemy refused dealt pretty heavily	

WAR DIARY
INTELLIGENCE SUMMARY.
(Erase heading not required.)

Army Form C. 2118.

308 Bde R.F.A.

Place	Date	Hour	Summary of Events and Information	Remarks and references to Appendices
LAVENTIE	1916 Oct 4th		B/306 Bde being withdrawn from the Group to take its place in a Composite Group formed. This Group plant is divided between A/308 and B/305, whilst covered by B/308. Capt. Twinn A/308 takes command of a Composite Battery in the new Group.	
	5th		M.T.M's cut wire in the early morning, having previously registered.	
	6th		Several working parties were fired on and dispersed during the day. Hostile Trench mortars opened fire in the evening and again in the afternoon but were quickly silenced by own batteries. Practically no hostile shelling on our front.	
	7th		Gun M.T.M's carried out the usual half hour shoot. The enemy replied with his Minnenwerfer. One of these was firing from Ht Thunderlin running East from THE WICK. Two hostile aeroplanes were visible, one of which flew over LAVENTIE.	

"A" Form.
MESSAGES AND SIGNALS.

Army Form C. 2121.

Prefix....Code....m.	Words	Charge	This message is on a/c of:	Recd. at......m.
Office of Origin and Service Instructions.				Date..........
....	Sent		..............Service.	From.........
....	At.........m.			By...........
....	To		(Signature of "Franking Officer.")	
	By			

TO { Left Group RA.

Sender's Number.	Day of Month.	In reply to Number.		AAA
* BMWO/48	7			

Reference	182nd	Inf	Bde	order
Number	43	2.45 am	is	ZERO
Time	aaa	acknowledge		

From 182nd Inf Bde
Place
Time 7-pm

J.P.Lorden Maj

VERY SECRET Copy No....7......
--------------------- 7/10/16.
Ref.Bde. Trench Map
   Area K.
                    OPERATION ORDER
                 by Lieut-Colonel F.H.Hilder;
                   for NIGHT OF 7th/8th OCTR.'16.
                 ----

1. A raid will take place on the night of 7th/8th Octr.1916,
   by a party of the 2/6th Warwicks Regt.

2.   The object is enter enemy trenches, kill
   Germans, obtain identifications, capture prisoners, and
   destroy his mine-shafts and defences.

3.   Point of entry - N.19.a.6.9.

4.   Zero time to be notified later.

5.   Watches will be synchronised at 11.15 pm.

6.   2/Lieut. Barnard, B/308, will act as forward
   control Officer.

7.   Reports to Group Headquarters (during operations
   and immediately afterwards).

8.   ACKNOWLEDGE.

                              Sidney F Simpson
                              Lieut. & Adjutant,
                                LEFT GROUP.

Copies to -
   1. A/308
   2. B/308
   3. D/308
   4. 61 Div.Art.
   5. 182 Inf.Bde.
   6. T.M's
   7. Diary
   8. File.

THE TABLE "A".

Time From	Time To	Battery	No. of Guns	Objective	Rounds	Rate of Fire
0.15	1.10	B/308	2 18prs	N.19.a.675.680	220-AX	Sec. fire 15"
–	–	–	2 18prs	N.19.a.800.775	220-AX	– – 15"
0.40	1.10	D/308	1 How.	N.19.a.375.600	60-BX	Gun fire 30"
–	–	D/308	1 How.	N.13.c.825.035	60-BX	Gun fire 30"
–	–	B/308	1 18pr (Enfilade)	Enfilade support trench in rear of point of entry.	40-A & AX	
0.30	1.10	D/308	1 How.	N.19.a.625.600	45-BX	Gun Sec. fire 30" for first 5 minutes followed by Gun Sec. fire 60" for rest of time.
0.40	0.50	A/308	1 18pr	N.13.d.175.060	10-AX	Gun fire 1 minute.
0.50	1.00	A/308	1 18pr	N.13.d.050.215	30-AX	– – 1 minute.
1.00	1.15	A/308	1 18pr	N.13.d.000.350 to N.13.d.150.475	15-AX	– – 1 minute.
0.00	0.10	M.T.M.	1 Gun	N.19.a.560.775		
–	–	–	1 Gun	N.19.a.620.875		
–	–	–	1 Gun	N.19.a.625.900 on wire.		
–	–	–	1 Gun	N.19.a.660.920		As fast as possible.
–	–	–	2 guns	Trenches round N.19.a.375.450		
–	–	–	2 guns	Trenches round N.13.d.125.225		
–	–	–	1 gun	N.15.c.980.230		
0.00	0.10	L.T.M.	1 Gun	N.19.a.375.640	20	Two per minute
–	–	–	1 Gun	N.13.c.875.125	20	Two per minute
0.10	0.15	–	4 Guns	N.19.a.375.640	120	6 per minute.
–	–	–	4 Guns	N.13.c.875.125	120	6 per minute.
0.15	1.10	–	2 Guns	N.19.a.375.5 640	440	4 per minute.
–	–	–	2 Guns	N.13.c.875.125	440	4 per minute.

The following are amendments to Table "A", already issued:-

The 1 How. firing on N.19.a.375.600 will start 10 minutes later, viz. 0.50 to 1.10. The one How. firing on N.13.c.825.035 from 0.40 to 1.10 will first fire on N.W. salient of Wick, N.13.d.0.3 to N.13.d.175.500 from 0.10 to 0.15.	Gun fire 30"

The 2 18 prs firing on N.19.a.800.775 at 0.15 to 1.10 will start 5 minutes later, viz. 0.20 to 1.10, and rate of fire to be increased to use 260 rounds instead of 220 rounds.

Sidney Thompson
Lieut & Adjutant,
LEFT GROUP.

7th Octr,1916.

1 copy to
A/308
B/308
D/308
R.A.
1&2 Inf.Bde.
File
War Diary.

308 Bde. R.F.A.   Army Form C. 2118.

WAR DIARY
INTELLIGENCE SUMMARY.
(Erase heading not required.)

Place	Date	Hour	Summary of Events and Information	Remarks and references to Appendices
LAVENTIE	1916 Oct 8th		A raid was carried out by 2/6th WARWICKS just NORTH of TRIVELET. This was supported by fire from 18pdrs & Howrs in conjunction with M.T.Ms. The raid was successful, our infantry gun the enemys trench, doing great damage and taking papers and identifications. No prisoners were taken.	See appendix B
	9th		No machine gun fire was encountered by the raiding pty. Hostile retaliation was not heavy. Bty continued shooting ten minutes after our fire had ceased. M.T.Ms shot for half an hour on Front Line. This was replied to by hostile T.Ms which were very active. D 308 specially placed on 4.5 How in position to enfilade two trench at N.14.c.7.4. 130 rounds were fired and a great deal of damage done. Enemy retaliation considerable with 4.2" and 77mm. also aerial Torpedoes.	
	10th		M.T.Ms cut wire at N.14.c.2.7. After firing bursts Bty were silenced owing to divert fire & enfilade.	

WAR DIARY or INTELLIGENCE SUMMARY.

308 Bde R.F.A.

Army Form C. 2118.

Place	Date	Hour	Summary of Events and Information	Remarks and references to Appendices
LAVENTIE	1916 Oct 10		R.3o.S again did good work on sunken ferry over 100 rounds.	
	11		Harassment fired on with good results.	
			A preparatory bombardment for a dummy raid was carried out by our artillery and T.M's, for the purpose of causing casualties to the enemy who having his supports the enemy did not fall up. The enemy answered but retaliated with T.M. 4.2's and Aerial Torpedoes. A large number of his minenwerfer were fired with the opening and consequently failed to explode.	
	12		Our T.M's fired during the day the hostile T.M's opened fire and were silenced by our fire after doing considerable damage.	
	13			
	14		Considerable movement was seen and working parties dispersed during the day. Our Batteries Co-operated with CENTRE GROUP in an attack on the enemy's trenches at M3c 9.5.	

WAR DIARY
or
INTELLIGENCE SUMMARY.
(Erase heading not required.)

Army Form C. 2118.

307 Bde R.F.A.

Place	Date	Hour	Summary of Events and Information	Remarks and references to Appendices
LAVENTIE	1916 Oct	15th	Considerable hostile movement was observed and parties dispersed. Our M.T.M's did damage to enemy front line and drew a considerable amount of retaliation.	
		16th	Five hostile aeroplanes crossed our lines but were in each case driven back by our anti aircraft fire. M.T.M's carried out half an hour programme, and drew very little retaliation. At 2.20 p.m. the enemy shelled LAVENTIE apparently registering the CHURCH. Seven 5.9 shells were fired. Old batteries in the Bray and Cath Brog fired on and into AUBERS, with the result hostile artillery ceased.	
		17th	Our M.T.M's carried out their usual half hours bombardment	
		18th	each day. Very little hostile fire and no unusual	
		19th	occurrences.	
		20th	Considerable aerial activity. Fire hostile machines being observed. MINENWERFER emplacement fired on at intervals.	

WAR DIARY
INTELLIGENCE SUMMARY
(Erase heading not required.)

Army Form C. 2118.

308 Bde R.F.A.

Place	Date	Hour	Summary of Events and Information	Remarks and references to Appendices
LAVENTIE	1916			
	6th	21st	A hostile aeroplane attacked one of our Kite Balloons north of ARMENTIER. The balloon was seen to fall to the ground in flames. Three hostile T.M.s opened fire, but were on each occasion silenced by our B.Batteries. Five hostile aeroplanes were observed doing photo work over our T.M.'s. Carried out a half hour bombardment doing much damage.	
	22nd		M.T.M.s again bombarded enemy lines.	
	23rd		At 11 p.m. a dummy raid was carried out. Bombardment and barrage was made by our 18 pdr M.T.M's and 4.5" H.O. with the object of inducing the enemy to man his parapet, and bring up supports. The barrage was lifted onto his supports and after a slight pause, air directed onto his front line.	
	24th		Very light. But there was practically no hostile fire. The enemy fired a large number of	

WAR DIARY
or
INTELLIGENCE SUMMARY.
(Erase heading not required.)

Army Form C. 2118.

3-8 Bde R.F.A.

Place	Date	Hour	Summary of Events and Information	Remarks and references to Appendices
LAVENTIE	1916 Feb 25th		A Lewis gun was fired at times at N.20.c.7.6. On Bn front as this had been one of our battries speed fire with shrapnell to kill any Huns around. Lt. Col. Willis proceeded to England, being handed over command of the 3-8 Bde to Major H.D. Day, & Col. Willis is struck off the strength of the Brigade	
	26th		Hostile artillery has shown unusual activity today. About 30 rounds of the shells fired were reported slim. The fire was principally directed on Red Lamp. His much trenches were inactive and we replied to their fire.	
	27th		Hostile shelling was again considerable on Red Lamp. Our T.M's fired during the day with good effect.	
	28th		During the morning the enemy fired a considerable number of rounds on back areas. At any rate of Russian 12 cm ammunition was fired. At 3.30 p.m a hostile bombardment of RED LAMP. salient	

WAR DIARY or INTELLIGENCE SUMMARY.

Army Form C. 2118.

3 o/8 Bde R.F.A.

Place	Date	Hour	Summary of Events and Information	Remarks and references to Appendices
LAVENTIE	1916 Oct 28	4ᵃ	—a.client started with various types of medium and light MINENWERFERS. About 250 rounds were fired. An organised shoot was given by this Group on entrenchments and tramways in N13d & N14c. At 3.53 p.m. Batthr control was given and a slow rate of deliberate fire kept up. At 4.30 p.m. hostile T.M's were observed, but started again heavy minute licks, with intermittent fire and artillery opened up on our reserve line CT's and Rue Tilleloy. Corps Heavy Artillery were called up and fired at fire latteria which were reported in action. Hostile activity ceased at 6.25 p.m. The withdrawal of the infantry of the 61 Div into Corps Reserve was completed on this date. The 5–6–59 minor took over the line previously occupied by 61 Div.	
	29ᵗʰ		Very quiet on Rt. front.	
	30ᵗʰ		A. Col. S.P. Foden assumed command of the 3 o/8 Bde R.F.A.	

WAR DIARY
or
INTELLIGENCE SUMMARY.
(Erase heading not required.)

Army Form C. 2118.

3rd Bde R.F.A.

Place	Date	Hour	Summary of Events and Information	Remarks and references to Appendices
LAVENTIE	1916 Oct 31st		An organised bombardment of hostile MINENWERFER emplacements was carried out at 2 p.m. The Corps Heavy Artillery and Heavy, medium, & light T.M's and 4.5 in H.rs all taking part. The enveloping trenches were subjected to sudden bursts of shfield fire by 18th B Allive during the bombardment. This was repeated from 3.15 to 3.30pm Great damage to material was caused the front line being drenched a N13 a.1.6. and N14 c.2.7.	

CONFIDENTIAL

WAR DIARY

308th BDE

1 - 30 NOV. 1916.

VOL. VII

CONFIDENTIAL

WAR DIARY
OF
308 Bde RFA

From 1st Nov. 1916 to 30 Nov 1916

(Volume VI)

[signature]
Comdg 308 Bde R.F.A.

WAR DIARY
or
INTELLIGENCE SUMMARY.
(Erase heading not required.)

308 Bde RFA Army Form C. 2118.

Place	Date	Hour	Summary of Events and Information	Remarks and references to Appendices
LAVENTIE.	1916 Nov 1	1.	From 2pm to 2.40pm enemy bombarded Shale mountings emplacement N13d. Nine by Heavy Artillery 4.5" Hows and 77. Fired mostly the 18pr subjected to enfilading bursts to keep hands away from the plate positions. The bombardment was repeated at 3.15 to 3.30 pm. Great damage was caused to a concrete dug out dugout and to parapet breached in one place. There was however no stockholding and very little hostile fire during the day.	SMM
	2.		Three hostile aeroplanes patrolled the line for over an hour. Now crossed the line.	SMM
	3.		Heavy and Medium trench mortars fired in cooperation with the artillery with good result.	SMM
	4.		The combined shoots with trench Mortars and artillery were carried out on hostile dugs, much damage being done to 12 enemy trenches. There was practically no retaliation.	SMM

WAR DIARY or INTELLIGENCE SUMMARY

Army Form C. 2118.

3rd Bd. RFA

Place	Date	Hour	Summary of Events and Information	Remarks and references to Appendices
LAVENTIE	1916 Nov 6th		One gun was withdrawn from road 15th Londons and fired on back areas during the night from an forward position with the object of worrying Delaney bn position to the enemy. Buildings at irregular intervals on heads and roads. Shelled to Kirchof at night. An unusual amount were again active.	9AM
	7th		Hostile batteries dispersed and wild firing carried on. One enemy aeroplane was observed flying well behind the German line.	9AM
	8th		Numerous parties of the enemy were seen and dispersed by our artillery. A Belied was evidently in progress and roads – CT's were subjected to bursts of fire to our batteries. Casualties were observed.	9AM
	9th		Enemy aircraft was much more active today. Three machines being seen one of which vainly tried to cross the line but was prevented by our anti-aircraft.	9AM

308 Bde R.F.A Army Form C. 2118.

WAR DIARY
INTELLIGENCE SUMMARY

Place	Date	Hour	Summary of Events and Information	Remarks and references to Appendices
LAVENTIE	1916. Nov 9th		A combined shoot by trench mortars and artillery totally destroyed the defences from M 24 d 6/12.4/1/2 to M 24 d 8.5. All the sand bag emplacements hereabouts were smashed in. 18 pdrs.	Appx
	10th		Several working parties were dispersed. A trench mortar bombardment was carried out in the afternoon. 8pm	Appx
	11th		There appears to be a quantity of water in the hostile trenches as on Five I Caned Cany opposite the trench mortars smashed up a crack dug out and a machine gun emplacement.	Appx
	12th		A machine gun emplacement at N 14 a 5.0 was totally destroyed by our artillery.	Appx
	13th		Trench mortars again bombarded every hostile	Appx
	14th		firing was carried out each day by T.M's in cooperation	Appx
	15th		with 18 pdrs. Working parties were dispersed.	Appx

WAR DIARY
INTELLIGENCE SUMMARY

Army Form C. 2118. 308 Bde RFA

Place	Date	Hour	Summary of Events and Information	Remarks and references to Appendices
LAVENTIE	Nov 19.16	16⁰⁰	Indian French Mortars again did good work, causing large white clouds of smoke with shots that appeared to have struck dug outs. Enemy parapet much damaged on both occasions.	SPM
		17⁰⁰		
		8ᵃ	Sections of the 6 How Bty were relieved by sections of the 6 (L) Div Art. as per Appendix. The outgoing sections withdrew to their Rest Area just south of BUSNES.	APPENDIX I SPM
		19ᵇ	The remainder of 308 Bde withdrew from their positions and joined the Brigade in the Rest Area. The guns of the 308 Bde were withdrawn in all cases.	SPM
		20ᵏ	The Command of the Group was taken over from Lᵗ Col S.P. MORTER by Lᵗ Col MELLOR, 308 Bde, Lᵗ Col MORTER returning to Brigade at the Rest Area	SPM
		21ˢᵗ	The Brigade resumed the march arriving at CAUCHY-a-la-TOUR in the evening	APPENDIX 2a SPM
		22ⁿᵈ	The Brigade resumed the march arriving at MAGNICOURT-en-COMTE in the evening	APPENDIX 2b SPM

WAR DIARY
INTELLIGENCE SUMMARY
(Erase heading not required.)

Army Form C. 2118.

308 Bde R.F.A.

Place	Date	Hour	Summary of Events and Information	Remarks and references to Appendices
	1916			
	Nov 23		The Brigade resumed the march arriving at BERTRANCOURT in the evening. Lt Col R.M. ORTER went forward from here to make a reconnaissance leaving Major N CHANCE in command	
	24th		The Brigade marched to AMPLIER.	
	25th		The Brigade marched to MARTINSART and took up their wagon lines here.	
	26th		The 2 S B ch took over 12.15 p.m. and 4.45 Hows in position from Lt Bde and landed over their 12. 18 pr and 4 4.5 Hows to Lt Bde at wagon lines W.16.27.7. Lt Col R.M. ORTER took command of the Group from Lt Col BROUGHTON midday 26th	HQ Post: 57.9.5.E 1/20000
	27th		Continued the policy of Lt Brigade by day and night firing.	
	28th		Weather very foggy and bad for observation	
	29th		Lt Bde Hows at the front.	
	30th		Ammunition allotment given as 1000 rounds 18 pr and 300 rounds 4.5 per gun how.	

SECRET.   Copy No......19......

APPENDIX I

61st. DIV. ARTILLERY ORDER NO: 21.

17.11.16.

1. The 6th. Div. Art. will relieve the 61st. Div. Art. in accordance with the attached Table on nights 18th.-19th. and 19th.-20th.

2. On the first night, all enfilade guns and 2 guns from the frontal positions will be relieved.
On the second night all remaining guns in frontal positions will be relieved.

3. Reliefs will not take place before 5 p.m.

4. One Officer and one sergeant for each enfilade section, and one layer per gun, will remain at the enfilade positions until the evening of the 19th. when they will rejoin their Units and go to the rest area.

5. The guns and equipment of the 61st. Div. Art. will be withdrawn and not handed over.

6. Officers and telephonists from relieving Batteries will arrive early on the 18th.

7. During reliefs, every precaution is to be taken not to make tracks in withdrawing guns from the pits, and in no case will horses be taken off the roads.

8. All Log books, photographs, diagrams of communications, trench maps, and drawings of gun pits, will be handed over and receipts obtained.

9. Wireless Masts and Wireless Operators will be taken, but the Spring Cart will be handed over to 6th. Div. Art.

10. All gun ammunition in pits, wagon lines and D.A.C. will be handed over to incoming Units at noon on the 19th. and receipts exchanged in accordance with para. 2, R.A.C.97/252 of 31st. October.
The 61st. Div. Art. will withdraw with empty echelons, and will refill in the rest area. The D.A.C. will march out with full establishment of S.A.A. and grenades.

11. The relieving Sections of the 6th. Div. Art. will arrive at our Wagon Lines on the afternoons of 18th. and 19th. about 4.0 p.m. The 61st. Division teams will hook into the 6th. Division guns and take them up to the positions, subsequently withdrawing the guns of the 61st. Div. Art. The Sections thus relieved will proceed to the rest areas and will be joined there by the remaining Sections on the following night.

12. The 6th. D.A.C. will relieve the 61st. D.A.C. on the morning of the 19th. at a time to be arranged between D.A.C. Commanders. On completion of reliefs the 61st. D.A.C. will withdraw to its rest area.

13. The 61st. D.A.C. will be responsible for ammunition supply up till noon on the 19th., after which the 6th. D.A.C. will be responsible.

(1)   14./

14.   The 61st. Division Trench Mortars will remain in the Line for the present, and will come under the orders of the 6th. Div. Art. at 9 a.m. on the 20th., the ammunition and Mortars being transferred to the 6th. Div. Art. at noon on 19th.   Subsequent Orders for their relief will be issued by the 6th. Divisional Artillery.   On relief the three H.T.Ms. and stores will be handed over to the 6th. Div. Art., the Medium T.Ms. being returned to 61st. Div. Art.

15.   The Command of Groups will pass on completion of reliefs.

16.   Group and D.A.C. Commanders will arrange with incoming Group and D.A.C. Commanders as to guides from each Battery and Section D.A.C. to conduct relieving Units to their Wagon Lines.

17.   G.O.C.,R.A., 6th. Division, will take over Command at 9.0 a.m. on the 20th.

18.   R.A. Headquarters, 61st. Division, will close at LA GORGUE at 9.0 a.m. on 20th. and will open at ROBECQ at the same hour.

ACKNOWLEDGE.

P.W. Meade

Major, R.A.
Brigade Major, 61st. Div. Artillery.

Issued at 7.0 a.m.

- - - - - - - - - - - - - - -

```
Copy No. 1     -        R.A. XI Corps.
 "      2     -        56th. Div. "G"
 "      3     -         "    "    "Q"
 "      4     -        6th. Div. Art.
 "      5 to 10        Right Group.
 "     11 to 14        Centre Group.
 "     15 to 19        Left Group.
 "     20         61   D.A.C.
 "     21              61 D.T.M.O.
 "     22 - 24         56th. Div. Train.
 "     25              10th. Squadron, R.F.C.
 "     26              5th. Div. Art.
 "     27              New Zealand Div. Art.
 "     28              A.P.M. 56th. Div.
 "     29              A.D.V.S. 56th. Div.
 "     30              XI Corps, H.A.
 "     31 - 32.        War Diary.
 "     33              File.
```

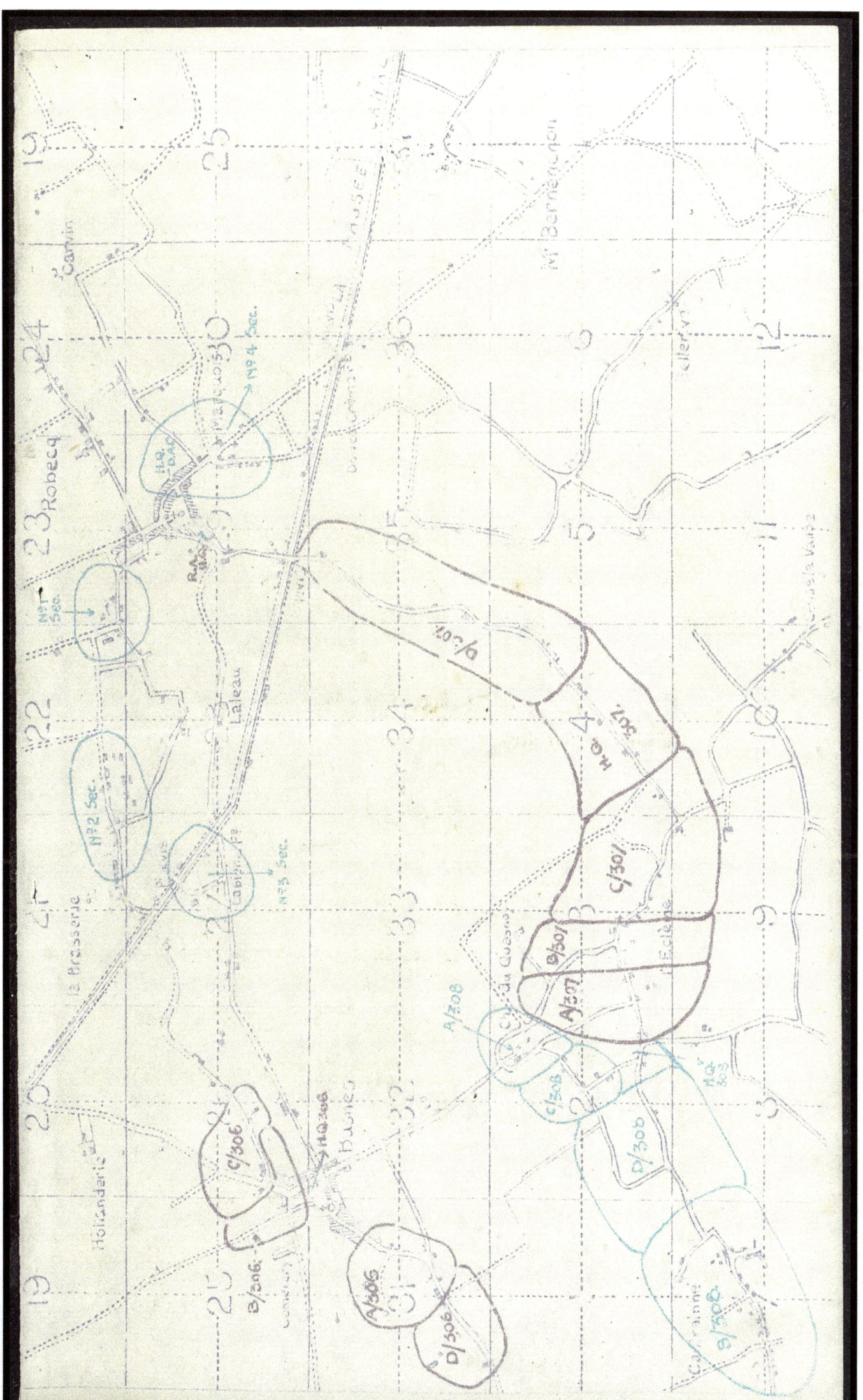

TABLE OF RELIEFS TO BE CARRIED OUT ON NIGHT 18th./19th.

Battery of 61st. Div. Art.	In position at	Relieved by	Wagon line to be occupied by Relieving Unit.	Remarks.
Sect. A/306.	M.34.c.5.4.	Sect. 21st. Bty.	R.9.b.6.3.	2 Sections A/306 on relief will withdraw to their Rest Area.
"	M.10.c.7.1.	"	"	"
Sect. C/306.	M.21.c.5.8. M.12.c.5.7.	Sect. 53rd. Bty.	R.3.d.1.2.	2 Sections C/306 " "
D/306.	-	-	Becomes vacant.	Will move complete to rest area on evening of 18th.
Sect. A/307.	M.26.d.5.5. M.23.a.2.8.	Sect. 110th. Bty.	R.5.b.6.7.	2 Sections A/307 on relief withdraw to their rest area.
Sect. B/307.	S.14.c.8.8. S.2.a.5.5.	Sect. 111th. Bty.	G.33.d.5.5.	2 Sections B/307 " "
Sect. C/307.	X.18.a.7.6. M.26.c.8.7.	Sect. 112th. Bty.	M.2.a.4.7.	" C/307. " "
Sect. D/307.	X.12.a.6.8.	Sect. 43rd. Battery.	R.10.b.2.5.	1 Section D/307.
Sect. B/306.	S.19.d.2.9. S.1.b.3.3.	Sect. 42nd. Bty.	R.10.a.2.6.	2 Sections B/306 on relief withdraw to their rest area.
Sect. A/308.	H.34.a.6.7. M.6.a.5.5.	Sect. 24th. Bty.	R.5.c.2.7.	2 Sections A/308 " "
Sect. B/308. 1 Gun.	M.11.c.4.3. N.2.b.9.8.	Sect. 72nd. Bty. 1 gun	R.4.d.5.3.	3 Guns B/308
Sect. D/308.	M.10.c.5.8.	Sect. D/38.	G.31.b.2.2.	1 Sect. D/308
C/308.		87th. Battery.	R.10.d.8.0.	Are relieved in their Wagon Line by the 87th. Battery on the evening of 18th. and withdraw to their rest area that night.

The 500th. Battery will remain in position. Wagon Line at G.11.d.8.8.

Completion of reliefs will be carried out on Night of 19th.-20th. on which night the remaining Sections of 61st. Div. Art. will withdraw to the rest area.

The Wagon Lines of 61st. D.A.C. are situated as follows:-

    H.Q.   L.26.b.1.2.
    No.1 Sect. R.11.central.
    No.2 "   L.36.a.8.2.
    No.3 "   L.26.d.2.8.
    No.4 "   L.27.c.2.7.

APPENDIX IIa

Copy No. .....11........

SECRET.

61 DIV. ART. ORDER NO: 22.

20.11.16.

Ref: HAZEBROUCK Sheet 5^A
1:100,000
LFS Sheet 11.

1. The 61st. Div. Art. will resume the March tomorrow the 21st. November in accordance with attached Table.

2. Billeting parties will meet the Staff Captain R.A. at Road junction RAIMBERT at 10.0 a.m. on 21st. November.

3. Supply Railhead for Nov. 21st. and 22nd. will be at LILLERS, Nov. 23rd. at AUBIGNY, and Nov. 24th. at FREVENT.

4. Immediately on arrival in Billeting Areas, Units will send guides to meet Supply Section A.S.C. at FOSSE. ½ mile S of Z in LOZINGHEM, to conduct Supply wagons to Units.

ACKNOWLEDGE.

[signature]

Major, R.A.
Brigade Major, 61 Div. Artillery.

Issued at.....4.30 pm.

```
Copies 1 - 5,   306th. Brigade.
   "    6 -10,  307th.    "
   "   11 -15,  308th.    "
   "   16 -20,  61st. D.A.C.
   "   21 -22,  No.1 Coy. A.S.C.
   "   23       First Army.
   "   24       XI Corps.
   "   25       61st. Division.
   "   26 -27,  War Diary.
        28      File.
```

APPENDIX 2a.

MARCH TABLE FOR NOVR. 21st.

Unit.	Starting Point.	Time.	Route.	Billeting Area.	Remarks.
306th. Bde.R.F.A.	Road Junction 400x W. of E in le CORNET BOURGOIS.	10.14 a.m.	LILLERS - BURBURE.	RAIMBERT.	
307th. " "	Road Junction 500x N. of R in LA NAVE R.	9.20 a.m.	LILLERS - BURBURE -RAIMBERT - AUCHEL.	CAUCHY-a-la-TOUR.	
308th. " "	Road Junction 750x E.N.E. of LILLERS CH:	9.30 a.m.	LILLERS - BURBURE -RAIMBERT - AUCHEL.	"	
61st. D.A.C.	BUSNES CH:	10.6 a.m.	BUSNES - LILLERS -HAUT RIEUX-LOZINGHEM.	AUCHEL.	
No.1 Co. A.S.C.	X Roads at ROBECQ.	10.10 a.m.	BUSNES - LILLERS -HAUT RIEUX-LOZINGHEM.	AUCHEL.	
R.A.H.Q.	R.A.H.Q.	10.25 a.m.	" "	AUCHEL.	

Copy No: **11**

APPENDIX II 6

S E C R E T.

61 DIV. ART ORDER NO: 23.

21.11.16.

Ref: HAZEBROUCK Sheet 5A.
LENS   "   11.
1:100,000.

1. The 61 Div. Art. will resume the march tomorrow, November 22nd., in accordance with the Table on the reverse.

2. Billeting Parties will meet the Staff Captain R.A. at the Church LA THIEULOYE at 10 a.m.

3. Immediately on arrival in Billeting Areas, Units will send guides to meet Supply Section A.S.C. at Cross Roads 1,500ˣ W.N.W. of LA THIEULOYE CH: to conduct Supply Wagons to Units.

4. Every Unit will be halted by its Commander at 10 minutes before the Clock hour, commencing at the first clock hour after the starting Point. The March will be resumed punctually at the clock hour.

ACKNOWLEDGE.

GW Meade

Major, R.A.
Brigade Major, 61 Div. Artillery.

Issued at **5.50 pm**

```
Copies  1 - 5,    306 Brigade.
  "     6 -10,    307    "
  "    11 -15,    308    "
  "    16 -20,    61 D.A.C.
  "    21, 22,    A.S.C.
Copy    23,       First Army.
  "     24,       1st. Corps.
  "     25,       61st. Division.
  "     26 -27,   War Diary.
  "     28, 22,   File.
```

MARCH TABLE FOR NOVEMBER 22ND.

Unit.	Starting Point.	Time.	Route.	Billeting Area.	Remarks.
306th. Brigade.	X Roads 400X N. of Y in CAUCHY-a-la-TOUR.	10.4 a.m.	FLORINGHEM - PERNES - VALHUON - THIEULOYE.	MONCHY - BRETON.	
307th. Brigade.	X Roads at FLORINGHEM.	9.30 a.m.	FLORINGHEM - PERNES - VALHUON - ANTIN.	ORLENCOURT.	
308th. Brigade.	"	10.7 a.m.	FLORINGHEM - PERNES - VALHUON - THIEULOYE.	MAGNICOURT - en - COMTE.	
61 D.A.C.	CHURCH of CAUCHY - a - la - TOUR.	10.25 a.m.	FLORINGHEM - PERNES - VALHUON - ANTIN.	La THIEULOYE.	
No.1 Coy. A.S.C.	"	11.32 a.m.	"	"	
R.A.H.Q.				CHELERS.	

SECRET   Copy No 6
         March Order No 5

(1) The Brigade will continue its march
    to-morrow as per attached R.A. orders
    and tables

Hqrs ⎫
C/308 ⎬ (2) Order of march as per margin
B/308 ⎟   Head of column to pass
C/308 ⎟
A/308 ⎭

(3) Cyclists, mess carts, and water carts
    will march with their batteries

(4) Baggage wagons will be
    brigaded and march under an
    Officer to be detailed from A/308

(*) Each Battery will detail 4 spare
    horses to accompany its wagons
    in leads & centres.

(5) Water-bottles are to be carried
    filled

(6) Batteries will be clear of their
    wagon-lines as follows:-
                              Continued

SECRET   Copy No 7

308th Brigade March Order No 3

Ref. LENS 11 1/100,000

(1) The 61st Div. Arty. will march as per attached orders and tables.

Hqrs.
C/308.
D/308.
A/308
B/308.

(2) The 308 Brigade will march in order as per margin.

(3) The head of the column will form up halted at fork roads by Brigade wagon-lines 500 yards WEST of "M" in MAGNICOURT. Time 7.0 am

(4) Billeting party and Interpreter will parade at Hqrs. at 7.0 am.

(5) C/308 will detail an Officer to take charge of baggage wagons

(6) Acknowledge

Copies to
1 to A/B
2 . B/B
3 . C/B
4 . D/B
5 War diary 22/11/16
6 "
7 File

Sidney Thompson
Lt. Adjt.
308 Bde RFA

SECRET   Copy No

308th Brigade March Orders No 4

REF. LENS 11. 1/100,000.

(1) The 61st Div. Arty. will march as per attached orders and tables.

Hqrs.
B/308
C/308
D/308
A/308

(2) The 308th Brigade will march in orders as per margin.

(3) The head of the column will form up facing SOUTH at road junction at first E of REBREUVIETTE. Time 8 am.

(4) Billeting parties and Interpreter will parade at Hqrs. at 8 am.

(5) D/308 will detail an Officer to take charge of baggage wagons, also 1 Shoeing Smith.

(6) Acknowledge.

Copies to:—
1 to A/308
2 " B/308
3 " C/308
4 " D/308
5 " War diary
6 " " "
7 " File

23/11/16

Sidney Thompson
Lt. Adjt.
308 Bde R.F.A.

CONFIDENTIAL.

WAR DIARY

308th I/BDE R.F.A.

From 1st December 1916 to 31st December 1916.

(VOLUME VIII)

Vol 8

WAR DIARY
or
INTELLIGENCE SUMMARY.
(Erase heading not required.)

Army Form C. 2118.

Place	Date	Hour	Summary of Events and Information	Remarks and references to Appendices
In the field	11.30		Carried out firing carried out in accordance with orders on Divisional Orders on Sibelen point. Daily Ammunition Expenditure. 17 par. 250 Pounds 4.5 Howitzer 150 Pounds.	8th Lt.
	12"		The Brigade Commander reconnoitred new positions for Brigade further in advance.	OM MH Lt.
	14"		Move commenced.	MH Lt. See app
	16"		Move commenced. Self Batterys in position and registered.	MH Lt.
	20"		Remaining day batteries in new positions registered. Brigade Headquarters moves to WONDERWORK South.	MH Lt.
	6		This 9th L.	8th Lt.
	27"		Brigade took over Left wing of Divisional front. Brigade Commander Brig.Col. D.F. Morley took over temporary command of Divisional Artillery. N.E. Lewis took over command of Brigade.	MH Lt.
	31"		Col Morten resumes command of the Bde.	Lt R.F.A.

Lt.Colonel B---
O.C. County — 308 Bde — RFA

SECRET.

308 BRIGADE R.F.A.

11/12/1916.

NOTES FOR MOVE.

1.   The Brigade will move from present positions to R.32.b.   Bde. H.Q. will be situated at R.32.b.0.4 on 20th inst. Battery Commanders will have gun platforms prepared at new positions for one section, move guns thereto, and register.   The remaining platforms will be proceeded with and completed before moving up the rest of the guns.   All moves and completion of moves to be reported to this Office without delay.

2.   All work from now onwards at new positions, must be continuous without fail. All accumulated materials at present positions will be transferred to new positions by means of tram routes.

3.   The tram routes are as follows:- Motor tram from present position to about X.7.b.1.9.   At this point, the horse tram route almost adjoins the motor tram route, and passing points exist on both lines.   Unload, and transfer and proceed to R.32.b.3.7.   At this point, a line will be laid under the superintendence of Major Day, along the contour to R.32.a.   In the first instance, B.C's will refer to Major Day for information concerning the use of the tram routes and arrangements for obtaining the use of trucks - mutual arrangements must be made so as to avoid as far as possible delays and waste of time.   It is most important that all ammunition on hand and materials be transferred..   A great deal of difficulty is being experienced in obtaining materials.

4.   The guns will be moved to their new positions via MOUQUET Fm. - THIEPVAL Road. This road must be very carefully reconnoitred *by officer from each battery* together with a senior N.C.O.   If B.C's consider this route practicable for G.S. wagons, it can be used to assist in transfer of material etc.   Only very light loads will be put on G.S. wagons.

5.   Each battery will provide 2 men for work on new tram line, and will report tomorrow, 12th inst., at 9.30 am on road by Medical Officer's tent; X.3.c.0.5, to Major Day - these men will have haversack rations daily, and will remain at the tram work till completed.

6.   Very careful arrangements must be made by B.C's with regard to supply of rations etc. at new positions.   It is hoped each battery will have 2 tram trucks.   A position at R.32.d. is pointed out as a place where the tram route crosses the road.   Supplies can be brought by road to this point and transferred to tram trucks, and from thence to battery positions.   B.C's must work out a careful time table and adhere to it. C/308 will continue to bring up Bde. H.Q. rations etc. Ammunition will be supplied from DONNETS POST by tram route.

- 2 -

B.C's should arrange to have from wagon lines as many men as can possibly be spared to assist in the work of preparation at new positions.

It must be borne in mind that the day and night programmes now in vogue at present in vogue must continue.

[signature]
Lieut-Colonel ;
Commanding 387 Brigade R.F.A.

CONFIDENTIAL.

WAR DIARY.

308th Bde R.F.A.

Mon Jan 1st — Jan 31st 1917.

(VI IX/)

Army Form C. 2118.

WAR DIARY
or
INTELLIGENCE SUMMARY.
(Erase heading not required.)

Instructions regarding War Diaries and Intelligence Summaries are contained in F. S. Regs., Part II. and the Staff Manual respectively. Title pages will be prepared in manuscript.

Place	Date	Hour	Summary of Events and Information	Remarks and references to Appendices
In Trenches	Jan 11	6.57	61st Div Art Order BYS 18/4 2Aug (E John) ob Montaudan 9.9 Self. Co-operation with 11th Division carried out in accordance with programme. Nightfiring on trenches & roads damaged in the recent bombardment.	
	12,13		Programme of operations as per BYS 18/9 F	
	14th		61st Div Art order 3.4. Carried out (programme attached)	
	15th		Brigade withdrawn from the line in accordance with Operation order No 9 (attached)	
	19th		Brigade moved from MARTINPART to MARTIN (interchanging with other Bdes)	
	20" 22"		Brigade moved from MARTIN to MONTIGNY-LES-JONGLEURS	
	23rd		Brigade moved from MONTIGNY-LES-JONGLEURS to MEULEY-LE-DIEN	
	24"		Brigade went into Corps Reserve	
	29th		Whole Brigade Army Corps/Army reserve training	
	27th		D/301 split up	

Wickwar Bray
Lt Col Commanding 301st Bde RFA

T2134. Wt. W708-776. 5000

WAR DIARY
or
INTELLIGENCE SUMMARY.
(Erase heading not required.)

Army Form C. 2118.

Place	Date	Hour	Summary of Events and Information	Remarks and references to Appendices
In the Field	Jan 1	-	Day & night firing carried out in accordance with Corps & Div'l Orders. Selected points. Daily Ammn Expenditure 18 Prs 250 Rounds 4.5 Hows 150 Rounds.	
	6	12-12th	Experimental barrage on Points – Trenches – O.G.1 + O.G.2 by 306 & 308 Brigades. (Copies of operation order N°8 attached A) This barrage was reported as being rather thin.	
	7		Lieut Gen'l Sir E.C. Bethune KCB accepts the Hon Colonelcy of the 308th Brigade R.F.A. (see letter B Attached)	
	9		61st Div Art Order 32 X day carried out (C) 308th Bde cooperating with 11th Div. Night firing on tender spots behind enemy line.	
	10		61 Div Art Order - Y day 33 - (D attached) - Night firing on Hostile Batteries & tender spots -	

www.ingramcontent.com/pod-product-compliance
Lightning Source LLC
Chambersburg PA
CBHW081429160426
43193CB00013B/2233